StartPoint: Parenting in "the White House"

Raising Empowered Young Women – Through a Father's Eyes

J. Edward White Jr.

ISBN: 978-1-7331-1060-0

DEDICATION

To my mom and dad, for being my StartPoint. To my girls, who are my
legacy.

CONTENTS

FOREWORD

My son authored this book, and he asked me to write the foreword. Reading the book brought back memories of my childhood and how my parents reared me. Born in 1945, I was the oldest of five children. I never knew my father, and my mother was rarely around. We all lived with my grandparents. By the time I was in the eighth grade my grandparents took over the parenting because my mother left the house. Daddy (my grandfather) died when I was in the ninth grade. At the end of my tenth-grade year, they removed my grandmother from the house because of her diabetes. A month later welfare picked us up and we were put in foster care.

As I look back, parenting between my grandparents and foster parents was not that different. During the early years with my grandparents, who were strict disciplinarians, if you got out of line, you got the switch. My grandmother took us to church on Sundays, both Sunday school and regular church. She made sure you got up for school every day, and you helped around the house after school.

Daddy was the man of the house, and he let you know that. He would tell you he was putting a roof over your head and food on the table. If you didn't listen to what they were saying, you would have hell to bear. As they got older, they were not as hands on. After my grandfather died, Granny's diabetes started getting worse. I gave her insulin before I went to school every morning; and when they put Granny in the hospital, it hurt very bad. My grandparents started the foundation on which I stand today. I loved them.

My foster parents were a mother and daughter, Miss Finch and Rose. They were also disciplinarians. We were in their care my junior and senior years of high school. They put a certain amount of structure in my life. They were Seventh Day Adventists, and they stressed church and education. Miss Finch had Bible study every Friday after sundown and church every Saturday. Rose stayed on me about school and keeping my grades up. She made sure I did my homework, and she would check it. This was what I expected and needed "parenting" to be. Both experiences as a child gave me some idea of how I would parent in my house.

After three years of military service and three years of work, God blessed me with four children between 1969 and 1972, two boys and two girls. Using my past experience, I decided early on how I wanted to raise my children. My wife Liz, their mother, and I decided to be partners in parenting. We would always have each other's back on discipline and the children would understand what family meant. I believed a good education was very important to their future. With that in mind, we had a priority list: (1) be respectful, (2) never lie to us, (3) give thanks to God, (4) education, (5) education, (6) more education and (7) always do the best job you can, no matter what. It seems that all four children took something away from their upbringing because they are living successful lives.

StartPoint is my youngest son's perspective of how a two-parent household can work. It's a book about a husband and wife putting a structure and system in place early in their children's lives and following a thought-out plan. It takes you through nearly two decades of their lives and the lives of their daughters.

The book gives you a bird's-eye view into how their parenting philosophy translated into raising their girls. It will take you from the time the girls understood how to say "no" to when they become young adults. It is a holistic parenting view teaching honesty, money management, athletics, education, sex and more.

The book tells you the life experiences of the girls, the life experiences of the parents, and how they put the time and effort in developing the girls into who they are today. The book is a great read; it holds your interest and informs at the same time.

Thank you, son, for asking me to write the foreword, and allowing me to share a little of my story.

James E. White, Father

PREFACE

This is a loving father's story about what my wife and I hold most dear, our girls. We believe they are our legacy and that our love for each other and them contributed to their success as children and as young adults. We are proud of what we did as parents, and this book serves as both an archive of experiences as well as a reference to help those interested navigate the twists and turns of parenthood.

I write about the parental approaches we used in raising two girls to be strong, confident, smart and beautiful young women. It spans multiple decades as the nearly twenty years of raising our daughters was preceded by the two decades of upbringing our parents did before we became parents. It is based on the premise that parenting is a strategic, multi-decade and multi-generational endeavor. It is bound by the sobering reality that our children's success or failure as adults are either "because of" or "in spite of" us as parents.

This book permitted us to tell our stories, share our views and assist families in raising future generations. Additionally, we hope this enables proactive parenting for all who have assumed this precious responsibility. From the stories, there are lessons that other parents can apply, if desired. We attempt to give our reasoning so that other parents can use our lessons as they manage the ups and downs of raising children to be functional, independent adults.

These stories are born from years of active observation and interpretation of my life—as a child, single adult and parent. It is a compilation of interactions and experiences personally and professionally, informed by my life and those of others, such as my parents, siblings, aunts / uncles and cousins. It also includes peer parental friends, older parental friends and co-workers' perspectives.

This book traces back to the upbringing of my dad because what he experienced and learned in his life contributed to how I learned to live my life—from childhood to adulthood to parenthood. I was directly or indirectly affected by the decisions that ultimately led to him marrying my mom and them having and raising me. How I was raised correlated to how I raised my own children. For many, particularly when the trace is negative, we hear "breaking the cycle." For *the White House*, we invest in perpetuating a legacy.

The decisions and actions of my father "set the tone" for the man, husband and father I am today. Despite not being raised by his father, he learned enough as a child and young adult that when he married my mom, and by the time they had me, he could lead our household. His example caused me to do the things I did as a father and contributed to me wanting to write a book about it.

My wife and daughters have ensured the stories and details in the book are as accurate as possible. However, as the author, the perspective is predominantly mine as both a father and head of household. Mindful, any joint parenting effort is a "we," but this story is filtered almost exclusively through my viewpoint. From my lens, I reveal a real story. The story is one that talks about deliberate actions to set the conditions for our girls to reach their full potential and realize happiness in all aspects of their lives. It is honest, candid and straightforward. The contents are not made-up but are based on either facts or best recollection. I offer opinions, techniques and philosophies that you can use as you deem appropriate.

What I am providing is not doctrine; it is not researched, and it is not a proven parental approach that guarantees successful children. I am confident enough in what we have done over the past 20+ years, however, to document it for others to read. I leave to you and those trained in the applicable areas to gauge the legitimacy of my views and logic.

I believe teaching a boy how to be a man is different from teaching a girl how to be a woman; but raising a child to be an adult is agnostic of gender. As parents, we teach them how to live in their truth, be genuine in private and public and have integrity. We teach them how to be accountable, respectable and honorable. We teach them the elements to attain peace, joy and happiness. None are specific to ethnicity, religion or sexual orientation, but all are what is demanded of parents when we decide to bring children into this world. If this responsibility is not recognized or understood at inception or at birth, it best be understood when those children begin to attain cognitive reference to their place on this earth. Apologizing for decades of ignorance or incompetence is difficult to accept, no matter how well-explained by the offender or empathetic the recipient.

We each have one life, with a discrete beginning and end. Your contribution to how your child experiences theirs is the most direct influence anyone has on another over a lifetime. For a parent to raise a child, they should know themselves, their issues and their character. To know these, a natural beginning is to recognize our own *StartPoint*. This book documents mine, and therefore, my children's.

With all that, my family and I encourage you to invest in reading and discussing the contents of this book with those you most love, as we truly believe you can find some value and it can be a benefit to you as a parent and your children.

CHAPTER 1
"THE WHITE HOUSE"

I believe the home should be a place of solace for everyone. Every member of the family should be able to find peace and feel comfortable expressing themselves in their home. Each of us, adults and children, need to have a place to rest and re-energize and share our successes and failures with those we love. It is my responsibility, along with my wife, to set those conditions. This does not preclude intermittent high-stress days; but the norm should be peaceful evenings with open, welcome and respectful interactions amongst the family and an environment that is sought out by each member to end and start a day.

That is the basis of reference for every member of our home which we call *the White House*. Within our house, each of us have a story. These stories capture our foundation, our frame of reference and the basis for our perspectives. They are tailored to our personalities, our relationships and our respective upbringings. My parents serve as my start point; my father's story shaped mine; his parenting defined my youth and influenced my adulthood and fatherhood. Similarly, my wife and I are our daughters' start point; and to understand our story, you should know a little about who we are.

About Me

My pen name is J. Edward White Jr., but most know me by "Eddie." If you are going to read about my opinions and beliefs, I figure you should know something about me. To know about me you have to understand a little about my upbringing.

I am the youngest child of Jim and Liz, born in 1972. I have an older brother and two older sisters. I was born in Pittsburgh, Pennsylvania but we moved, in 1978, to Salix, PA, a middle-class suburb about ten miles outside of Johnstown, PA. My high school, Forest Hills, is in Sidman, PA where the Johnstown Flood Museum is. I don't recall much prior to 1978 except that I was a little edgy as a young tyke. One could say it was due to the environment in which I was growing up. Others could say it was because my sisters kept causing me to run home to stay out of trouble, and I was getting tired of it. Either way, the move to Salix was a big deal, and was a signature decision by my father that put his family in a different setting.

That setting included a very limited number of minorities, and that is being generous as essentially my family was the only black family in the neighborhood. At the time, my brother was the first black student to graduate from Forest Hills, and I was the last. My sisters went to the vocational school. As you would expect, growing up as an extreme minority influenced my view of aggregate ethnicities. Growing up in an almost exclusively white school system, where I had the full spectrum of those who liked and disliked me (though more liked), I learned that everyone had individual characteristics that could not easily be categorized exclusively based on their skin complexion. It also taught me that to exist, and potentially excel, as a minority I must understand the unique situation I am in at any given time or place.

I became a Herschel Walker fan in 1979 / 1980. For those who don't know, he is considered the greatest Georgia football player of all time. And why is that important? Well, that love of Georgia football directly led me to apply only to the University of Georgia (UGA) and being accepted early during my senior year in high school in 1988. I graduated from UGA in 1993 with a Bachelor of Science - Chemistry degree, a commission into the Regular Army and no debt as I had earned a 3-year ROTC scholarship.

I was raised in a loving, caring and demanding household. I played basketball and ran track in high school, holding school records in hurdles and making the Pennsylvania State Track and Field Meet (States) as a senior. I maintained about a 3.5 GPA with a college preparatory curriculum, including acing chemistry, which is why I chose that major at UGA. I didn't date any girls in my high school for various reasons and didn't have sex before college. I didn't drink before I was twenty-one, and I never did illegal drugs. I was never abused in any form; and I flirted with the law on one occasion, but thankfully nothing came from it. I walked the line many of us walk as teenagers, even though I was a "good kid," prayer, love and God kept me from spiraling down a path that may have stunted or delayed the successes I achieved as an adult.

My parents demanded good grades, and if it wasn't cool to be smart, then you weren't cool—but we weren't going to be nor act stupid. They expected you to work for what you earned; and if you didn't do well, then learn how to work harder or smarter, but work would be the common denominator. I respected all those I interacted with, adults and peers; and although I was black, it didn't fundamentally detract from my social experience in my predominantly white school or neighborhood. I visited my twin cousins for two weeks every summer, and I routinely went to church with my aunt and uncle. My family wasn't deep into the church, but in some form or fashion religion was always in my life. I had great relationships with my cousins, aunts and uncles growing up, and knew family meant something. I had a mean streak in me, likely from my time in Pittsburgh, but I never got in a real fight growing up. I, in many respects, was a typical middle to upper middle-class kid. I was immersed in a predominantly white social setting, though my core and extended family was a traditional strong black male-led one where many of us played sports, went to college, worked steady jobs and even owned small businesses. So, the "black" family was not negative—it was welcome—and the "white" school /

3

neighborhood was also positive. I did sports and other activities in Johnstown, where most of my social interactions with other black children who weren't family occurred, as well as Lynchburg, VA where my dad grew up and we would visit every year.

While I had several experiences in middle and high school, there was one that truly defined my perception of reality. I call it my re-evaluation period, and it mostly shaped my adulthood up until 2012, when I had my second major personal life-reflecting experience. It was the first time I was forced to reconcile what my perception was and what reality was presenting; and since they were not the same, I had to decide how to make the two fit.

My perception was based on burgeoning success in track and a self-confidence in all things that bordered arrogance. I was doing things as a teenage boy that were not right, but okay in my mind. I was confused about my emotions, my relationships and had a naivety that masked the reality that truly existed around me.

What marked the beginning of this period was the district track meet in the spring of 1988. At the time, I was the top 110 and 300-meter hurdler in our district. I had won every track meet that season; I was getting local press due to my success, and I was a clear favorite to make States. I was not really practicing as my natural ability allowed me to succeed while enjoying track "practice." I flirted with girls, played basketball (half-heartedly), did running and hurdling drills, and otherwise clowned around until the actual meet, where I often easily won. Our track team was not good. We did not have an actual track so we had to pull equipment out of the shed and find places to run and workout in and around the school. Our football coach was our track coach because we could not find anyone truly qualified after the previous coach left. Since I was the best on the team, I was not overly pressed to change my ways. So, for me, track life was good. This was especially important because I was the point guard on what likely remains the worst basketball team (by record) in school history just a few months prior.

So that was track and all was "good in the neighborhood." I was also aggressively trying to make money. I did not get an allowance, so I was perpetually lacking money. I did side gigs to mitigate this problem. I created and sold t-shirts to other "elite" hurdlers in the district, for one. I also used my father's alcohol collection to my benefit. Separately, I was challenged to date anyone in my school; but that did not preclude me from wanting to. This was a major conflict as my best friends were beautiful and smart girls (one was our class valedictorian), but we were only friends. As you can imagine, this was difficult for a young teen boy. There are certainly many factors, including my ethnicity, but the reality caused me to be emotionally pained. I did well in school. I had a great reputation as a student-athlete. My family's reputation was outstanding as my parents, brother and sisters all did well in their respective areas. As a family, we had no issues, rumors or negativity with or within our community. So, despite my individual money, emotional and relationship stresses, on the surface I was as good a kid as any parent could hope for a sixteen-year-old boy.

But as most know, what is done in the shadows eventually comes to light. That saying soon became my reality. The sequence traced back to a weekend request from some "friends" to get alcohol from my father's collection. During their visit, our dog ran upstairs and I went to get him as I was the only one home and wanted to keep him close. What seemed trivial at the time turned out to be a critical actuality a few weeks later.

The scenario that ultimately defined my "re-evaluation period" began in earnest once the district track meet arrived. Upon arrival at districts, my track coach informed me the district had not received the times he submitted. Therefore, I was not rated as the #1 hurdler in the district, but merely as a qualifying hurdler. This was inconsequential for the 110-meter hurdles, but it put me in the worst possible situation for the 300 meters. For the 300-meter hurdles, they only did two heats with the overall top three times earning spots in the state meet. Since I was only a qualifier, I got the worst lane (inside lane) in the first heat (separate from the other fastest hurdlers). The result was a 4th place finish overall. I literally defeated those in my heat by 100 meters; but when compared to the final heat racers, my time did not make the cut. As such, any aspiration for States in the 300 ended quickly. It was discouraging, but not catastrophic. Although I was better in the 300, I did not consider it my best race. I still had the 110-meter hurdles, in which I made the finals and had a preferred lane.

Then the business side of Districts started to influence this meet. I was busy finding and selling my t-shirts throughout the day. This caught up to me as I was rushing to get ready and be in place for the actual finals race. I was also a notoriously bad starter, but this rarely became a factor due to my abilities from hurdles 3-10. But due to me rushing around, when the race started my legs felt heavy; and I started slow (once again). In expected fashion, I started to close the gap on the field around hurdle number five; and then it happened. As I was passing the hurdler to my right, his arm came under my arm and threw me off balance. Apparently, we were so close that either my arm was in his lane or his arm was in mine (I think his was in mine for the record). Regardless, the incident caused me to nearly stop cold to catch my balance. This momentary pause resulted in me only getting up to 4th place, and so ended any hopes of reaching States as only the top three make it. For me, it was crushing. Not because I worked so hard to make it, but because it seemed like it was a given. I was riding high all year, and I was recognized as a "big-time" performer. In less than twenty seconds, all of that ended. I went under the bleachers and cried, and tried to figure out how this happened.

That was only part of the "beginning." The next, more ominous part, occurred that night. I was in my room stewing on the results of the day, numb from it all—almost zombie-like—when my mother told me the police were at the house and wanted to see me. I went to the living room, and they explained that a kid fell out of an apartment window and was injured. They discovered he had both drugs and alcohol in his system. They got word that he may have gotten the alcohol from me. The next few moments would have lifelong reverberations; I did not fully comprehend the gravity of my next words, but I knew what I was going to say. The easy part was I was already in a zombie-like state, so although it was an anxious moment, I was calm and steady. I told the police that I had come upstairs to get my dog and left them in the basement. They must have taken the alcohol while I was upstairs. The police, due in part to the standing of our family, did not press. They thanked my parents and left. My parents, especially my dad, looked at me and did not say a word. I zoned it all out and went back to my room, slowly realizing how close I was to a very bad situation.

It was that day, and those events, that caused me to fundamentally re-assess how I was living, what I was doing, how I viewed the world I lived in and the reality of being me. I went deep into thought and began analyzing everything about my life, my school, my friends, my decisions, people's reactions and whatever I could dissect. I re-evaluated all things associated with my life because what I had experienced shook the very foundation I had known.

To this day, I consider that time as my "Abraham moment." I know God invested in me early in my life, even before I had truly invested in Him. For those who are not familiar with the Abraham reference, you can read Genesis 20:2. In general, there was a time when he lied about Sarah being his wife because he feared what would happen when he was asked by a band of men due in part (my interpretation) to the circumstance he created by not adhering to what God had directed. Afterwards, God intervened and resolved the situation. When the men asked Abraham why he lied, he admitted he had done so out of fear. God still blessed Abraham and used that experience as a teaching point. To me, I was Abraham. I created the situation by doing wrong; and, when confronted I feared the consequences and chose self-preservation. God has used that to further his Kingdom through me. At sixteen, I did not grasp all of that (at that point I did not know Abraham as I had not read the Bible). I just knew I had to figure out how not to experience that again. After the re-evaluation, I changed my attitude about many things, some of which were good, some not as good; but all of which were to better serve me and my aspirations. This affected all who met me in some form; it dictated decisions I made, it affected how

I performed in college and in the Army and it affected relationships immediately thereafter as well as after I graduated from college. It had a profound impact on all I did beginning my senior year in high school, and it would be that way really until 2012 when I reached another point of redress … but that would have to be a different book.

After college, I spent the next 25+ years in the Army, ultimately attaining the rank of Colonel (O-6) and serving in various places across the country and world. I have led hundreds of soldiers, sailors and airman in varying capacities, working in joint and multi-national organizations and affording my children both the pros and cons of relative instability.

So, that is the primary author of this book, a college graduate, an Army officer, a husband and a father by the age of twenty-three. I did not live in a demented, violent, dysfunctional world growing up. My parents have been married my entire life. We have family dinners and vacations, attend siblings', nieces' and nephews' achievement ceremonies; and we love each other as you would want / hope. My upbringing was healthy, fostered freedom of thought and realization of aspirations within reason. It is what I wanted for my kids when they were growing up, save some of the edginess and "fine lines" I walked if they could be prevented.

About My Wife

This section is Vambie's story, written by her but tailored to my perspective for consistency to the reader. It is of equal importance to my background as Vambie orchestrated our parental approach from day to day, and masterfully managed the girls' lifestyle and the household. Vambie was not a secondary figure in the upbringing of our girls. Truth be told, she was the centerpiece around which everything revolved. I subscribe to the saying "happy wife, happy life," and learned that the better the kids, the happier the mother / wife. So, to fully appreciate the chapters of this book, you should understand some things about her.

Her history is relatively simple. She was born and raised in a town in Georgia, but she did not know her biological father. However, she was raised in a two-parent household for the first twelve to thirteen years of her life because her mom got married soon after her birth. She has a younger sister and brother. Her mom left her father during her middle school years. Her family received food stamps throughout her youth because her father had a seasonal job. After her dad and mom got divorced, her mom worked at a grocery store in town. Her mother then got a full-time position on the military post after a few years. They didn't have much; but for her, "you don't know what you don't know." They went from one trailer to another. Her great aunt had a trailer off a dirt road her uncle used, but he said her family could move there. At the height of her teen years, there were at least five of them living in a three-bedroom trailer on Cay Road. She and her siblings went to her father's place every weekend until into her freshmen year in high school.

Her escape from all that was involved in living in the country was learning how to play the clarinet in elementary school. She then went behind her father's back and learned how to play her brother's saxophone. Afterwards, she tried out for the middle school band on her brother's instrument. She eventually got her own saxophone for free, and band became her outlet from Cay Road. She joined the jazz band in middle school and from there, she joined the high school marching band. She was Vice President of her class for the last three years of high school. She dated in high school, but nothing serious. She was a smart butt (academically and socially) throughout school. She was always told "you are going to college," but she was not exactly sure how—though that was "the plan." She was voted class clown, she got decent grades and nothing catastrophic stunted her growth during her youth. She was blessed with the opportunity to go to college, literally. She arrived at Albany State University on a "prayer ride" with her mom and her aunt as they had no money and no financial aid packet. They sat in front of the financial aid building the Sunday she was supposed to sign in and waited. She can't remember the woman's name, but that day the woman "coincidentally" stopped by her office to get some forms to finish after church. Despite only stopping by for some files, the woman sat there with them and walked through all the necessary paperwork telling them that by Thursday Vambie would be in school. For the non-believer, understand that prayer works! Vambie enrolled in the Winter semester of 1989 and officially graduated after the spring of 1994 although she completed requisite course work in December 1993.

After graduating from Albany State, Vambie was commissioned as an Active Duty Army officer. However, her military experience was not necessarily straightforward. Vambie initially joined the Army reserves in 1988 and went to basic training at Fort Jackson, SC. After basic training, she went to San Antonio, TX to be trained as a Combat Medic. She later joined the Reserve Officer Training Corps (ROTC) through the Simultaneous Membership Program, so for a time she was both enlisted in the reserves and training to be an officer in ROTC. Nearly six years later, Vambie was commissioned and went to Fort Bliss, TX as a 2nd Lieutenant. She finished the Officer Basic Course and was then stationed at Fort Polk, LA in August 1994. Her sponsor got in contact with her and they planned to meet when she arrived at the base. On that Monday they met, and she was invited to "Taco Tuesday." This is important because on that day, although she didn't know at the time, she met Lieutenant Eddie White. She was standing outside waiting on her sponsor when this guy (that would be me) walked up to her to introduce himself. She thought no more of it until two weeks later when we met again at a party and as they say, "the rest is (and was) history."

We met that night and talked in general about a million things. From there we went on maybe two or three dates. We moved in with each other in October, we got officially engaged in December and we married in March 1995. We had our first daughter in September. While we had been on our own for some time, nothing prepares you for raising children. So, we needed to get ready quickly; and she understood that all plans go out the window when you hear that first cry. She had said during her early twenties that she didn't want kids, so finding out she was pregnant was a total shock. Yes, there were a couple of days of denial until she got confirmation from the doctor. After acceptance that it was happening, she understood "you have nine months to figure it out, and time starts now."

We discussed a lot of things to include what we thought about having kids, even though that was not what she had planned. We loosely talked about discipline, activities and religion, and what we thought it would be like to raise a boy versus a girl. Even though we discussed some topics, kids will show you that even the best laid plans can, and will, go awry. In her view you must be flexible, acknowledge when the load is heavy and know when to let things go. However, under no circumstance do you show a split defense to your child / children. We agreed to that joint front, hands down. The reality, after children, is you talk about the livelihood of your child more than yourselves.

From there we began our journey of parenting together. Vambie selflessly invested energy in raising the girls and keeping a healthy and functioning household by loving each of us in her own way. She set her expectations and made it known if they were being met or if improvement was needed. She served in the military until our second daughter was born, then left on her own terms honorably. Afterwards, she focused exclusively on raising two little girls to be strong, independent and confident young women.

About My Family
As the basis for this book is a healthy family conducive for raising children, allow me to describe mine. We refer to ourselves as "The Core 4"—me, Vambie, Jaelin (oldest daughter) and Jaleah (youngest daughter). As written in the previous section, Vambie and I met during our first duty location in Louisiana, and we got married within a year. It was clear to me then, as is the case now, that she is smart, confident, independent, loving and spirited. She is someone who challenges me, holds me accountable, demands that I realize my potential and supports my role as head of household. She is my true soulmate. She complements me perfectly and I am blessed to have her in my life "until death do us part."

Prior to getting married, we openly discussed children. I wanted them, if one then two. We did not have in-depth talks about our philosophies and parental tenets; but in learning about her, I was comfortable with raising children with her. This is fortunate because the same time we got engaged to be married, she got pregnant. We had our oldest and youngest within eighteen months of each other.

Our family has lived in Alabama, Germany, Kansas and Virginia. As a guiding family tenet, Vambie has a signature saying: "I don't deal with mess." This is indicative of her and the family's aversion to drama. This caused us to function in a candid, honest and direct way. We deal with people and situations as they are, not as desired or imagined. We talk about the realities of life, consequences of poor decisions and the power of keeping your word.

Our daughters are best friends. The oldest, Jaelin, started kindergarten at four-years-old while we were stationed in Germany. This caused her to be younger than her peers throughout school, and we considered holding her back upon our return to the states to attend first grade. Although we ultimately did not hold her back, we were concerned about her maturity and how she would adjust socially when she eventually got to high school. In general, she worked hard in all grades and excelled academically. Her outgoing personality allowed her to get along with her peers even though she was typically younger. When she struggled, she was forced to put in the work to achieve the requisite standard—whether in school or sports. She was a high-level soccer player, but she suffered two torn ACLs. She graduated high school with a 3.7 GPA, and she was a four-year letter winner in soccer despite the injuries. This enabled her to earn a partial soccer scholarship to Howard University. There she studied International Business, earned paid internships during her college summers and dedicated hours volunteering with the Boys and Girls Club in the greater Washington D.C. area. She ultimately earned a business analyst job with a Fortune 50 company immediately upon graduation.

Our youngest, Jaleah, tested as "gifted and talented," and was old relative to her peers throughout school. Due in part to her high IQ, she had minimal struggles in high school; she graduated with a 4.1

GPA and earned a semester's worth of college credit. She studied accounting at Eastern Michigan University and while earning her master's degree, tested to be a Certified Public Accountant. She was a high-level gymnast; but like her sister, tore her ACL. The strain and subsequent tear cost her two years in the sport she loved; and she was unable to attain an athletic scholarship. However, due to her success in high school, she earned academic scholarships.

In any marriage, the leading and partnering of the parents is a delicate balance built on mutual respect and trust. In as much as I assumed the responsibility to head my household, Vambie allowed it. She trusted me, enabled me and empowered me. Without such support, my impact on the girls would have been significantly reduced—and this book would likely not have been written. I know all that is written occurred because I experienced it; and, collectively, the Core 4 confirmed it. However, I acknowledge all that is contained is not all that occurred.

No single perspective can fully capture all sides of a collective experience; and as the single author, this introduces an inherent slant. As such, Vambie's influence on / within the home was more prominent than what the book documents. Using a *Matrix* analogy, if I was the Architect then Vambie was the Oracle. The breadth and depth of Vambie's involvement in each of the girl's day-to-day life causes her role in how the family functioned to be under-represented in the written stories. In more instances than I am aware, my involvement was after Vambie foresaw the situation, preemptively planted a seed for me to act upon and / or took initial action until I could more actively be involved. In certain cases, Vambie did things and gave me credit (almost always without me ever knowing).

Vambie's decision to leave the Army and focus on raising the girls enabled me to excel professionally, while still doing all I write about in this book. Her decision permitted the girls to exist in a perpetual and tangible state of love and attention. Vambie was there when they got ready for school in the morning, and was home when they returned from school. Contrasted to my two to four hours a day when I got home, which varied based on their sports schedule and any given job. Then I had extended time on the weekends, also tempered by their competition and activity schedule. Therefore, the contents of this book, and the things I did to affect my daughters' growth, are a fraction of the explicit and implicit things Vambie did for them during their upbringing.

She invested fully in the whole of *the White House*—the energy, inter-relationships and respective individual aspirations. Vambie was aware of my mental and spiritual state and even more so attuned to the girls' mental, emotional and physical health. She willingly sacrificed professional aspirations for the family. She also recognized the girls needed to see she was not "just a stay-at-home mom" (whether fair or unfair), so she got her master's degree. Vambie freely absorbed everyone's stress and fear, while simultaneously amplifying our respective joys and successes.

All of this contributes to the mindset of our family. The Core 4 takes precedence over all others. We demand openness and honesty, tempered when they were young children, less filtered once they became young adults. We will not compromise our relationship, our love, our respect or our appreciation of each other for any reason. We are committed to each other's growth and maturity in all facets of life—whether mental, physical, emotional, spiritual, financial, in relationships, school or career. We laugh and cry together; we share in each other's successes and challenges; and we know if or when needed, you can trust the family will be there to support. Each of us understands that we represent our family name wherever we are, and we have pride in knowing we are a part of *the White House*.

Setting Parental Conditions

The first year or so after Jaelin was born we did like most parents probably do: wing it. Which means, do the best we could from day to day, be very careful about it, marvel at the miracle that is in our arms and pray we don't screw this up. But after a couple of years, and with a second child, the fascination of parenthood quickly shifted to figuring out how we would actually parent. Since it was not formally established beforehand, we had to explicitly or implicitly determine how we would collectively raise our kids. For us, there never was a doubt that both Vambie and I were "all in." This demanded we invest ourselves physically, mentally and emotionally in our girls and how our household would function. Initially both of us worked, and this meant sharing responsibilities across the board. After Jaleah was born, we decided that Vambie would not work unless she wanted to and we would adjust our lifestyle accordingly. This was a significant adjustment, but we decided the benefit of her staying home worked best for us. I managed the money, and we made compromises. We had to keenly balance wants from needs and short-term from long-term goals; but in general, money was never a major issue. Each of us brought our own views and attitudes to the table. We were independent but respected the inherent co-dependence of marriage and parenthood. Having a daughter within the first year, followed by another less than two years later, we quickly got into figuring out how we would parent together.

In 1998, I had a revelation from a more senior Army officer and father who caused me to realize that raising my girls could not be done by happenstance, that "playing by ear" was not the most effective approach. He shared that he had not invested enough time and energy when his daughters were young due to working long hours, deploying (sometimes voluntarily) and otherwise not being present. Unfortunately, it did not hit him until they were teenagers, at which time he essentially missed his daughters growing up and there was nothing he could do. I didn't understand initially since my kids weren't even four-years-old at the time; but soon thereafter, I realized what he meant. His level of influence by the time they were teens was so reduced that he could not truly shape them and experience things like young parents imagine. From this, I decided I would begin early in my girls' lives to establish a solid foundation for multiple decades of development and future adult child-parent relations. His story resonated with me and directly affected my family.

A key part of setting our conditions was establishing common philosophies. We agreed on general approaches on how we would raise our girls and manage our household. I can't recall all of them, but I provided some of the core ones we had early on:

"As best as possible, prevent any life-altering catastrophe from happening during upbringing."

"Raise kids to be functional adults."

"High self-esteem is important, especially for girls."

We agreed on these as a set of ideas to guide us. Each had practical applications to how we taught our girls, made decisions and set conditions within our household.

Here is how we applied those tenets in our day-to-day parenting:

"As best as possible, prevent any life-altering catastrophe from happening during upbringing." – Have active, open and honest discussion about the consequences of doing the most high-risk activities such as having sex, experimenting with drugs or underage drinking. We were also aggressively involved in understanding their relationships and communications with friends; we sought to meet the parents of friends, we required "checking in" and we intermittently checked up on what they said was occurring during key shaping years. Further, the threat of embarrassment of not adhering to our rules was ever present and understood as a realistic action.

"Raise kids to be functional adults." – Have mature, advanced talks about post-high school / college responsibilities and challenges. We used failure as opportunities to teach. We did not shy away from adult topic areas, and we set conditions for non "yes-no" situations to be dealt with positively. We treated the girls "age-appropriate" and we increased levels of responsibility as they got older. I paid them for making my lunch, and we mandated money management. We talked about them living on their own, paying bills, owning a car or home; and we did not avoid the costs associated and limitations based on salary.

"High self-esteem is important, especially for girls." – We emphasized the importance of self-confidence, and we empowered them to make decisions and be held to account for those decisions. I wrote letters to accentuate how proud I was of them and highlight their accomplishments. I told them they were beautiful on the inside and outside; and I told them I loved them, hugged them and kissed them good night. We told them not to accept abuse from anyone, especially a man. We specified the types of abuse (sexual, physical and emotional); and we explained that no form of abuse was tolerable. We taught them to not accept someone cheating on them, regardless of how good they may appear. We emphasized they represented our name in all they did, and we told them to be proud and set high expectations which they could fully realize if they worked hard enough and demanded from themselves what was required.

These examples transcend any single action; but we actively sought to implement our philosophy at each age, so the desired attributes could come to fruition. It was important to have them, trust them and practice them in some way.

These philosophies were primarily mine, but Vambie supported them. However, there were instances where our individual philosophies were markedly different. They emerged as the girls got older and we dealt with different situations. The way she viewed certain occurrences and their importance would be different from mine at times. Regardless of how similar or different our approaches were, we had to reconcile those differences so that the girls' perception of expectations was consistent and clearly understood.

My general view of day-to-day parenting was to establish a "left and right limit" with a fair amount of latitude; and only when those limits were pushed or crossed would I more actively engage in resolving that issue. Counterpoint, Vambie had an "everything matters" approach, and she actively engaged our girls on nearly anything that did not align with her expectations. Thus, whether it was cleaning the house, not turning in a homework assignment or giving a vague answer to a pointed question, any instance would incite a level of "parenting investment" that exceeded mine.

These differences created instances of conflict and disagreement between us. There are a few examples that come to mind. One includes when and how to intervene when they were in high school and we received progress reports. As you know, progress reports are not final report cards, so it is up for interpretation about how important they are. When the respective progress report was "below standard," our responses were very different. I downplayed the importance because to me it was about the actual report card. We could talk about what needed to be done to improve, or why they had a given mark, but ultimately it was not a significant emotional event. Conversely, Vambie treated the receipt of the progress report as an interim report card, carrying the same importance. This perceived importance generated intense discussion and accountability akin to the actual end-of-semester grade. Another example was the importance of doing, or not doing, household chores. This was somewhat important to me and essential to Vambie. Whether a major chore or a trivial clean-up (my words), failure to complete generated a level of parental investment that far exceeded my threshold. These came up at varying times and ages, but they are indicative of our differing views. If we were to dig deeper, one could derive our views from how we were raised, the value placed on any given activity or action, and what that translated to when we became adults. Resolution, in general, began with recognizing when and why these approaches conflicted. This was easier said than done. I had to recognize the subtle or distinct differences that come along with our varying approaches and then, which may be the most challenging, figure out the best way to resolve.

We attained resolution in various ways depending on the circumstance. For me, after recognizing the differences and understanding the conviction of Vambie's approach, I begrudgingly accepted that I would not change her methods. This was important in that she recognized that she would not change mine either; therefore, we did not argue whose approach was right but moved to creating a complementary dynamic that reduced friction between us and with the girls. This was not easy. During a situation that I clearly would have handled differently, I quietly observed or consciously removed myself—and I allowed Vambie to address it in her way. As the years passed, an important realization emerged that helped me deal with any frustration I may have had in how the situation played out—I am not always right (nor is my approach). There is great value for our girls in experiencing each approach throughout their lives. This is one of those benefits that the kids will realize when they are adults. Exposure to the unique personalities of Vambie and I would reinforce each of our characteristics in different ways. The reality is, whether positive or negative, they adjusted to those parental approaches and that, in and of itself, helped shape their personalities later in life.

To attain complementary parenting approaches, we had to honestly and openly acknowledge these crossroads then assess the significance of the impact; how we interacted with each other and, more importantly, how we balanced each other when interacting with the girls. Respecting these differences in private helped yield a unified and consistent front in public / with our girls. From there, the girls adapted, and we could apply more focus to their development than to arguments about how "I would have done that differently."

Recognizing Personality Traits

A key leadership tenet is knowing yourself so you can effectively lead others. To help develop this tenet, the Army offers the Myers-Briggs personality test. Both Vambie and I took this test during our military careers. Once we had our girls, we consciously sought to identify our respective traits in them. This spanned many years as mine or Vambie's characteristics would emerge based on the setting or circumstance. Obviously, our girls represent us, the good and the bad; so, tracking those traits and accepting the genesis to determine how to best address a given situation was vital.

Personality traits, or characteristics, derived from us and realized in our girls, played a key role in how effectively we managed our household. I am primarily my father's son. The way I think, analyze problems, determine solutions and interact with others is based, in many ways, on my dad. I am also a momma's boy, to a certain extent; so, my sustained energy level at work and home, as well as my extroverted tendencies, come from her. Similarly, my girls carry in them aspects of me and Vambie; so, before I chastise them, I reflect on where that characteristic came from.

First, we must understand and accept that we as parents have characteristics that either physiologically, psychologically or conditionally will be passed on to our children. Secondly, it is on us to identify which attributes our children pick up and adjust our parenting approach accordingly. Our girls demonstrated different attributes as they grew and matured. As such they viewed situations and reacted to them based on either one, or both, of our personalities. We actively invested time and energy to understand which traits, and in which combination, each of our girls got from me and / or Vambie.

For our girls, we determined Jaelin to be much more me than Vambie; while we estimated Jaleah to be more Vambie than me. These are "guesstimates" agreed upon by me and Vambie. The specific attributes were played out either in school, athletics, social settings, relationships or in how they dealt with situations. This allowed for candid discussion between Vambie and me regarding how a certain trait could be addressed based on where it was derived. These ratios played out in some distinguishable ways. For Jaelin, based on our alignment of similarities, we could easily carry on a conversation. She would naturally pick up what I was putting down, track the salient points and figure out how that applies to her. Such was not the case with Jaleah. When we talked, I sometimes had to be more demonstrative, give analogies or diversify the examples to make my point. I also was not as certain she picked up my points. But we knew this early on, so I became more patient and deliberate in my conversations with Jaleah because I had to be.

Understanding where the traits derived from and how each child demonstrated them was only part of the equation. The next was determining how to create a scenario that benefited the respective child. The next few paragraphs are examples of how the personality traits traced to the girls and how we practically addressed each situation:

Learning Style: Throughout elementary school and early into middle school, it became apparent Jaelin was challenged with reading comprehension. She demonstrated this in her grades from school, discussions with her on why she was struggling and parent-teacher conferences. Once identified, Vambie and I had several talks about how to help her (i.e. tutor or special reading program) since the normal in-house solutions were not producing the desired results. At one point, Vambie asked if I had this issue as a kid as she did not recall personally having a reading comprehension problem at that age. I could not recall, so we called my parents who said I also struggled when I was younger in the same area. From this, we assessed my approach to dealing with this problem over my life, at least through college, and weighed if this was something that over time could be overcome naturally. We also did not blame Jaelin for this shortcoming. Instead, we viewed it as a passed-down problem we collectively needed to address. Ultimately, we decided to continue with our in-house approach, but we increased the amount of time and energy we would invest to help her improve reading comprehension and subsequently how to express that in writing. This meant three or four re-dos of homework assignments at times over multiple years as we had to set the tone for our commitment to resolve. It took several years before she cleared the hump; and although a special tutoring program could have resolved this challenge sooner, for varying reasons (i.e. her schedule and the cost) we decided it could be handled internally. This was not an easy decision, but we tried to include all factors: cost, our time, her resolve and consequences. It was, ultimately, a family solution that demanded collective patience and work.

Admitting Error: Vambie and I have several characteristics that are fundamentally different. One of these is how we respond to problems or questions posed to us. For Vambie, she is very quick-witted, with a high IQ and aggressively assesses situations and answers questions. This aggressiveness sometimes yields quick answers with or without all the information being known. Therefore, the probability of being incorrect is higher, but her willingness to accept her error and apologize for any mistake is very natural. Conversely, I am fairly analytical in my approach and very deliberate. This causes slower response times, but relatively speaking, lower error rate. However, it does not eliminate the error possibility. A negative trait of mine, unlike Vambie, is I am reluctant to apologize or admit when I am wrong. This is an acknowledged flaw, and Vambie has learned to handle or accept this flaw throughout our marriage. The problem is Jaleah has a "less than ideal" combination of these traits. She has a high IQ and is quick to respond to questions. However, she was reluctant or unwilling in some instances to apologize when that quick response was wrong. Since there is an error rate, whether high or low, this was problematic. Therefore, we tried to impress upon her the importance of recognizing and admitting fault. During this endeavor, we discovered that recognition of being wrong was not the main issue—admitting it was. The perception that she was expected to always be right over several years created a personal belief that she could not admit if / when she was wrong, whether known or not. After many open and honest discussions, some positive, others not so positive; some quiet and others not, eventually there was significant improvement. This started as a two-person talk between me and Jaleah. It then became a family approach to break the perception and make her feel less pressure to be the "smartest who always has to be right." I cannot singularly identify the breakthrough that led to the improvement; but holistically, we doggedly addressed this problem over several years in ways that would not compromise the positive traits and mitigate the "less than ideal" attributes.

Who Decides: Recognizing the "dominant derived traits" was important in establishing which parent had the "expertise" in dealing with certain topics that would or could have long-lasting impact on a given child. This understanding was a central factor in deciding which school Jaelin would attend after the opportunity arose to transfer her to a different elementary school without consequence. After moving to Virginia from Kansas, Jaleah's "gifted and talented" status was reaffirmed, and she was placed in a dedicated gifted program with peer classmates. This put her in a different elementary school than her sister, but also gave us the option to move Jaelin to this elementary school, albeit not in a gifted program. This became the basis of "who decides" as the transition to the new school was particularly difficult for Jaelin and Vambie. Jaelin came home crying nearly every day because the teacher had a unique approach, one she had difficulty adjusting to—and the strain of the environment was taking a toll. This stress resonated with Vambie, and she was supportive of moving Jaelin to the other elementary school with her sister. However, in my view the struggles caused by the teacher's techniques would ultimately benefit Jaelin; and therefore, I did not believe a change should be made. This disagreement introduced multiple philosophical conflicts and a passionate argument between me and Vambie. The final decision was, in part, based on my views of the long-term benefit of forcing Jaelin to adjust to the teacher despite clear short-term pain and frustration. The basis for my position was from my personal shortcomings and this situation, in my opinion, could provide an opportunity for the potentially "negative traits" to be lessened in Jaelin. To Vambie's credit, she deferred to my perspective; and after several months of adjusting, Jaelin benefitted significantly from the teaching style and subsequent teacher recommendations that proved important later in her academic career.

Ultimately, Vambie and I decided to run the house following a basic model: establish our philosophies which served as our parenting goals for when our girls became young adults; decide on what we need to do and how we would enable those philosophies (what parental approaches to apply); tailor the approach for each girl based on their strengths, weaknesses and personality. This was the model with the respective plan, fully acknowledging that executing this plan would be a challenge in and of itself. For us as parents, success would be defined by how close to our aspirations our daughters were when they became young adults. I encourage every parent to follow a similar model, recognizing that raising children without any plan causes us as parents to "wing it," hoping the results are positive after nearly two decades of effort.

This chapter detailed the basics of *the White House*, who we are and what we aspired to achieve in practical terms. As a more scriptural goal, in our foyer for years we had a plaque hanging that captures the essence of what every family should strive to attain (from the LIGHTHOUSE CHRISTIAN PRODUCTS CO).

Our Family

We will love and accept *one another.*
ROMANS 14:1, ROMANS 15:7, 1 PETER 1:22, 1 JOHN 4:7

We will pray for *one another.*
PHILIPPIANS 1:3-4, 1 TIMOTHY 2:1, HEBREWS 13:7, JAMES 5:16

We will tell the truth *to each other.*
EPHESIANS 4:25, COLOSSIANS 3:9, 1 PETER 2:1, 1 PETER 3:10

We will be kind *to one another.*
ZECHARIAH 7:9, COLOSSIANS 3:12, 1 THESSALONIANS 5:15

We will bring joy *to each other.*
PROVERBS 15:30, PROVERBS 17:22, PROVERBS 23:25, PHILEMON 1:7

We will serve *one another.*
ACTS 20:35, JAMES 1:27, 1 PETER 4:10, 1 PETER 5:5

We will be patient *with each other.*
1 COR. 12:12-25, EPHESIANS 4:2, COLOSSIANS 3:13, JAMES 1:19-20

We will comfort *one another.*
2 CORINTHIANS 1:3-7, GALATIANS 6:2, 2 THESSALONIANS 2:16-17

We will forgive *one another.*
LUKE 6:36-37, LUKE 17:3-4, COLOSSIANS 3:13, 1 PETER 3:9

We will be generous *with each other.*
PROVERBS 22:9, ACTS 2:42-47, 1 TIMOTHY 6:17-19, 1 PETER 4:9

We will honor *each other.*
MARK 9:35, ROMANS 12:10, PHILIPPIANS 2:3, 1 PETER 2:17

CHAPTER 2
CRITICAL SHAPING YEARS

The first few years after Jaelin was born, we were typical loving parents—we sang, read and counted; helped her stand, walk and talk; hugged, kissed and played baby games with her to foster that parent-child bond. We did all we could to make her happy. The fragility of a young baby, coupled with newness of parenthood, created a fresh, caring and nurturing household. With our kids being less than two years apart, this environment blended together up until Jaelin was close to four-years-old. Since Vambie and I held similar views on child discipline, we instituted the "spank your kids" approach when we deemed they could differentiate between yes and no. So we incorporated more "child discipline" around the respective age of two or three, while still fostering that caring environment.

This balance of "baby nurturing" and "child discipline" in the very early years of parenthood was fairly straightforward in our household. When they didn't do what they were told or tried to hide something that they knew was wrong, even at three- or four-years-old, we took disciplinary measures whether it was raising our voice, taking toys away, not allowing them to leave their room or go outside—or as a last measure, spanking them. The focus was on developing mental and motor skills and imprinting upon them a sound foundation of parental love and care that subconsciously would carry throughout their lives.

It was when Jaelin was around four-years-old that I came to realize happenstance parenting was not an ideal approach. A few years later, when she turned six-years-old, is when the shift from "baby nurturing" and "child discipline" transitioned to "raise kids to be functional adults." This, on the surface, seemed early. I mean what can a six-year-old really understand about adulthood? I was convinced, however, that this was the time, and as I look back I am even more certain that roughly five / six-years-old to twelve / thirteen are the critical shaping years.

I do not know what child psychology research yields regarding the most critical time in child development, and I don't believe we did anything unique during the very early formative years. The point of debarkation began when our girls attained the mental capacity to comprehend, at least in part, the explanations about becoming a functional independent adult. In our house, that was "go time."

A central theme to my early messages was self-esteem, consistent with one of our main philosophies (high self-esteem is important, especially for girls). I was impressed by Vambie's self-confidence and what that enabled her to be and achieve. Therefore, I made instilling this in the conscious and subconscious of my girls an early priority. Self-esteem is confidence and satisfaction in oneself; and this trait influences decisions and actions, particularly when circumstances are less than ideal. The benefits of attaining this trait are numerous: improved communication skills, development of coping mechanisms, self-respect, demand for quality and high standards from themselves and others, just to name a few. Conversely, low self-esteem can cause self-destructive behavior and preclude achievement of one's full potential. For me, it was critical that each of my girls realize the long-term value of themselves and have confidence in who they are, the decisions they make and what they will accept.

Establishing this trait was not a single lesson. It was one we routinely reinforced during both success and failure over multiple years. One of the sustained ways I communicated these type of messages was by sharing *life nuggets* with my girls. This was a commonly-used term I created when I had lessons to teach. It had clear connotations that over the years the girls accepted, understood and even referenced. Leading in with the term helped get them into a mindset as they knew it was time to listen and learn as some life nuggets took longer to explain than others, and they wouldn't know until completion. Whether deep or shallow, including the whiteboard or happening while driving in the car, life nuggets were an integral part of their upbringing. Although at times nuggets may have been something they dreaded, over the years, they came to recognize them as opportunities to spend time with their dad and to learn more about life.

The number of life nuggets I shared certainly numbered in the twenties or thirties, many of which singularly I cannot recall. I started them during the critical shaping years, but they span well into high school and even their early college years. I noted topics based on experiences from work, interactions with friends, watching TV shows or movies, attending church as well as successes and ethical dilemmas. I attempt to capture some of the more noteworthy ones throughout the book, mindful that some were done on the whiteboard because it was the most effective way to convey the message. I have scattered examples of life nuggets throughout the book to give an appreciation of the subjects, but the timing varied.

Life Nugget: Self-Perception *– This was a whiteboard session done during the critical shaping years as I wanted to instill this lesson sooner rather than later. I graphically drew out the layers between how you perceive yourself and how others perceive you. It started with how you feel when you look in the mirror: how confident you truly are, how you believe you are without any caveat—essentially, how do you view the true you? This includes your skin color, your personality, your joy, your weaknesses and your strengths. Then the layering starts—how do those closest to you, who* *matter the most, view you—and how similar or different is that from the "true you?" How do you affect that difference? Do you actively try to influence that, and is that perception positive or negative? Another layer is friends then acquaintances like classmates and subsequently strangers. With each view you are in different settings, and based on how you present yourself, they interpret your character, personality, confidence, weaknesses, or limitations through that lens. After the graphic was depicted, we actively discussed how misperceptions can affect their confidence, how they can be dishonest with themselves and how the façade they present at school or in social settings shapes their reputation, whether positive or negative. It was not a simple nugget, but it was central to establishing self-esteem and self-confidence by teaching them to know themselves and owning that reality, while simultaneously acknowledging that what they do, say, how they act and perform directly affects how others perceive them.*

Cumulative Effect

During these early shaping years, the cumulative effect was the principle reason I invested so heavily in talking to my girls about all that I believed they may experience throughout their lives, from middle school to retirement. I obtained this view after several experiences with teenagers in other settings where they presumably had sound and timely advice but with minimum effect on the respective outcome. As the other teens were not my children, and I had limited involvement in their upbringing, I decided early on to implement an approach where I would introduce and build upon significant lessons over several years for my kids. This would increase the probability those lessons would stick and they would factor into their decisions, opinions, attitude and actions. To achieve the desired effect, I had three pillars:

Identify Critical Lessons: The lessons I chose were completely subjective and inherently based on my life's experience.

I kept the lessons to a small number so I could routinely apply due focus. I presented my most critical lessons under the saying / acronym of "don't be SAAD." The acronym SAAD represented S – (no) Sex; A – (no) Alcohol; A – (no) Abuse (physical, mental, sexual); D – (no) Drugs. I routinely referenced this saying, explained the significance of each in detail and reinforced each tenet over several years. I had other lessons that were important; and although I did not deem them critical, I found that they also arose multiple times over the years. I was fine with repeating the value of both the critical and less critical at every opportunity.

Opportunities to Reinforce: As the girls experienced more situations, both positive and negative, we actively listened to when one of those critical, or important, lessons could be introduced into the conversation. It could have been directly or indirectly tied to a given area, but as often as possible we exploited the opportunity to reinforce the respective message. For me, the "don't be SAAD" mantra was based on proactively avoiding things that shake the very core of your life and demanded an extreme reaction. The ramifications of reacting the wrong way or contrary to what we taught them in any of those situations, in my view, would be catastrophic. Therefore, when discussion arose about friends who experimented with drugs, or were drunk at a given event, the situation allowed for further conversation on the consequences physically, psychologically or legally—depending on the topic.

Consistency: The essential points and their respective importance remained consistent. Consistency was needed to create the desired effect. The message may have expanded or included caveats, but it did not fundamentally change. The risk of altering those messages was that a state of confusion may be created, and actions may be taken that were inconsistent with what I had been teaching. There are two other sections in this book dedicated to the "don't be SAAD" mantra, to include the graduate edition, which exemplifies how I applied caveats to this critical lesson.

Both Vambie and I actively observed and discussed how we believed the girls adhered to our lessons. We acknowledge there is no absolute certainty that the effect took hold, but we invested time and energy to identify genuine indicators to best measure the effectiveness.

The broader application of the cumulative effect is in the early education of what we deemed to be characteristics of functional independent adults. This early education dictated introduction of unconstrained topics in varying forms and forums: Saturday morning talks between the four of us, whiteboard talks to graphically make points, long drives in the car or dinner conversations. Topics spanned whatever we thought of at the time or knew needed to be explained—personal accountability, societal dynamics, cultural perceptions, buying versus renting, government versus corporate jobs, salary versus hourly wages, money management, integrity, religion, relationships and education, to name some. We did not singularly discuss any topic. We took advantage of each opportunity. We did not avoid multiple explanations in short periods of time. These topics formed the foundation for future reference as they matured, so more was better. Since they were relatively young, we tempered the explanation accordingly, but we avoided no topic under the premise "until they were ready." In my view, during the shaping years, they may have only understood some, but they listened to most. Since it could be factored in their life, it was worth it.

Philosophically, the generational gap becomes more prominent the older the kids get, as such the inevitable "parents just don't understand" phase emerges. Therefore, the most significant early impressions are during the single-digit years when it is not perceived as painful when the "parent talk" comes about. This factored into my overall basis for considering these "critical shaping years."

This aggressive approach subconsciously planted the seeds that our girls can talk to us about anything. The various talks spanned ten to twelve years, and they allowed for in-depth discussion when the girls experienced more or had questions they could not answer. As none of us could know when these life situations would emerge, the girls' preparedness to deal with or talk about those situations were, in part, based on how and when we introduced the given subject.

A key consideration for pursuing this aggressive topic introduction approach is making complex topics simple for the age of the children. Talking about salaried versus hourly forms of income, home ownership or cost of living based on regions of the country to an eight-year-old depends on how well the parent understands the topic, the aptitude of the child and how well it is explained. Although some topics are decades away from being relevant to a pre-teen, others will be realized in years or months. A standing approach I personally used is, at a minimum, talk "one level" ahead of the child; and as often as possible, talk "two levels" ahead. This meant when the girls were in elementary school, I did not talk about the challenges and pitfalls of elementary unless forced to address specific situations—that is the "same level." Instead, I talked about what middle school may entail, and how the situation changes when they go to their next school—that is one level ahead.

In the above example of talking about middle school while in elementary, we talked about the changing class structure, such as multiple teachers versus a single teacher, dropping from "top of the ladder" in elementary to "bottom of the ladder" in middle school and how class subjects become more diverse. Further, with a two level approach, we began active and practical talks about high school and what may occur in that environment. By taking this tact, we reduced the number of arguments regarding how "out of touch" we were since they cannot comprehend high school in elementary and therefore, could not challenge our views. Additionally, I built on the conversation when the situation arrived "in-year" because we had brought up that potential circumstance three to five years prior. In day-to-day living, we talked in-year experiences that came to fruition but remained vigilant in projecting future challenges to reduce stressful conversations later. We sought non-crisis discussion, so we could posit thoughts to help prepare them, and us, for the unique strain we would likely encounter at the next level. Examples included when we would allow the girls to date, future sport participation criteria (relative to cost, injury and time) and how far from home we would allow the girls to travel for college. In general, Vambie focused on in-year while I concentrated on the next one or two levels, with each adjusting the key points of emphasis in real time.

These next-level discussions were common in routine conversations as it was very natural in our household. However, we included the "middle school to retirement" subjects as well when the forum was most conducive. Additionally, I included routine "look-backs." It was important for us to highlight successes achieved, challenges overcome, accepting responsibility for stellar accomplishments and dealing with criticism without them losing confidence for less than stellar undertakings. The conversations were personal, held multiple times over several years, and were one of my critical responsibilities as a parent. All of these conversations were interwoven into both next-level and longer-range subjects to establish this sound foundation.

As mentioned, if a topic was relevant to living, it was on the table. We felt we could not avoid certain matters or wait until they were older because we believed the results could have been counter to what we desired as parents.

Next are some examples of those topics and how we went about shaping the girls' views:

Money Management - Paying them to make my lunch: I had a discussion with both my girls in the summer of 2006 (nine- and eleven-years-old) asking if they were interested in getting paid to make my lunch every day. The reasoning was to expose them to what it meant to earn money and subsequently manage that money over several years. This was not chore-based but explicitly money management-based. Initially, it was hourly-based, meaning if I was out of town and no lunch was required, they received less money for the month. Additionally, if they forgot, I simply made lunch myself; but I also deducted that day's income. Later, we renegotiated to salary-based income, whereby they earned a set amount whether I was in town / needed a lunch or not. This salary-based "contract" also caused a zero tolerance for not making my lunch any given day. If during summertime, for example, they forgot, I would wake them up to make my lunch. It was a demonstration of pros and cons of salary-based employment, in tangible terms. By the time they were in high school, they would hear me getting ready and, if they had not made the lunch the evening prior, come downstairs to make it before I left. The contract ran through each respective girl's high school graduation, so six and nine years respectively. It offered practical discussion on quality of service, spending habits and value of savings. This was reinforced in high school and served as a common reference regarding any money management discussion through college and into young adulthood.

Confidence in Math / Science - Summer Class Program: A recognized issue for many children is a fear of math and / or science. I did not presume my girls would be immune to this just because I am a scientist. Because this fear directly contributes to struggles in the classroom and potentially an aversion to pursuing careers in these types of fields, I took a very proactive approach. I created and held summer programs in algebra, geometry and chemistry when the girls were in elementary and middle school. I did this over a four-to six-week period for one to two hours a week based on my personal selection of topics. These were not voluntary lessons; and although the girls were initially reluctant, after a couple of sessions, they enjoyed the time with me and I with them (for the most part). When we had family visits, similarly aged nieces / nephews also participated. This served multiple purposes: increased confidence that they could succeed in respective classes, decreased need for assistance once they started taking the classes, overall increase in self-esteem due to subject-specific confidence and success in the given class. This also served a longer-range goal of enabling my girls to pursue math / science-based college degrees. Despite these classes not always being welcome, the chance to interact with my girls and affect how they approached academic challenges would be valuable later in their lives, including college.

Summer Reading Program: Vambie led this program, and my only involvement was the family dinner we did at the end of summer before school started as a reward. Vambie either selected the books (number and title) or allowed the girls to select, and she gave them a timeframe to complete. In some instances, she had them write a summary or they talked about the books. This was also not negotiable, and she used it to keep them moderately engaged during the time between academic school years. It also afforded opportunities to talk about lessons learned from the books.

As the girls approached the teenage years, the strong communication foundation that started when they were six-years-old truly came into effect. This foundation of mutual trust helped bridge the "my parents don't understand" phase that can be the most frustrating for both parents and children. Unfortunately, there is no cure-all for this phase. We mitigated much of this frustration by staying one or two levels ahead, but the reality of parent-child friction was unavoidable.

As the girls neared the end of these critical shaping years, the energy, time and topic management became more prominent. The ages from eleven to thirteen during middle school began to create situations that were more complex and pressed their ability to understand them. At the same time, the talks about broader life topics did not wane. As they got older, depending on the subject, the resistance to such discussions increased, to include the amount of attention the girls offered, freely or begrudgingly. I did not relent despite their belief that they had it figured out. Conversely, when necessary, I increased my aggressiveness because I believed their reliance on us for explanation and context remained high; and their ability to understand the points, although better than when six or seven, was still challenged despite their perception as teenagers.

I decided early on that the shaping years are the foundation for child-parent communications and relations for decades to come. From my experience, open and unguarded conversations would likely decrease during the teenage years; therefore, the most open, honest and influential time for us to affect our girls was between six and thirteen. During this timeframe, Mommy and Daddy are the center of their world—and what we say matters. This influences how they act and what they tolerate, which invariably shapes them without their knowledge. The time spent engaged with them will mean a lot. We understood quality was important, but we could not undersell quantity. As parents, we did our best to set the conditions to maximize both quantity and quality during these early stages; and we deemed we could compromise quantity later when competition for their time would be more intense and the perceived importance of our lessons reduced. To me, the gratification from being a parent is the highest during the shaping years, including less conflict and attitude from the children, more respect for the presence of the man and woman who created them and an open mind that recognizes there is a lot they as children don't know and the ones who know the most are their parents. Although I expound on the specific teenage year challenges in the coming chapters, there are stories to be shared about what we dealt with during these critical shaping years.

Father – Daughter Time

I believe there was a reason God made me a father of daughters vice sons. There are things in life that we have no control over, but God enables us to excel in every endeavor if we listen to His guidance and are diligent in our stewardship. As parents, we are stewards of God's children; and He, as the creator, has deemed we are fully capable of raising them. He decided I would have two girls, and it was not for me to complain about not having boys, nor to give less of myself to my daughters because they are girls.

I firmly believe the cross-gender relationship is as important as the same-gender relationship throughout childhood development. Over time, I have discovered there are various approaches fathers have used raising their daughters including no physical discipline, deferring key decisions almost exclusively to the mother, viewing / treating them as "girly girls" and not pushing for them to participate in sports that would help instill that competitive drive. I will admit, I was not a father who avoided physical discipline, who deferred my decisions, exclusively raised my daughters to be "girly girls" or tried to dissuade competitiveness. Balance across the board created experiences that were both good and bad for my two girls, relatively speaking, of course.

The bad, at least to them at the time, was the approaches I used to discipline them. They were spanked by me as well as Vambie. I voiced my frustration and / or dissatisfaction academically, athletically and / or socially when I experienced it. I set and shared expectations for them that, when not met, caused me to voice my disappointment. I did not treat them with "kid gloves," I engaged, confronted and demanded a level of performance from them that my father before me had established and I willingly perpetuated. However, I sought to not be overbearing about it. I tried to use a tone that would not generate contempt for me, but I did not soften my approach due to that concern. I wanted to teach them not to compromise other facets of life to achieve perceived excellence exclusively in one. I tried to educate them on citizenship, treating people with dignity and respect, having values and being grateful for opportunities made available to them based on family, friends or their hard work. This was not always pleasant, but some lessons are not meant to come across as "happy and glad."

I think it is fair to surmise my girls considered the above instances as bad initially or at the time of being disciplined. I also believe they would be much more appreciative of those experiences when they became young adults (in talking to my now young adult children, I was correct). On the other side of the coin, we had our fair share of occasions that were mutually viewed as good both initially and thereafter.

In my view, investing time and energy early and often allows for more selective investments later. Creating the pre-cognitive environment, even the portion where they will minimally recollect, is included. I spent time counting to them before they could talk and helping them stand before they could walk, but the more cognitive father-daughter time started when they were around three- to five-years-old. While stationed in Germany, we did walks to the local park and fed ducks, sledded down hills during the winter and walked downtown to get ice cream in the summer. These were vague memories when they got older, but such activities established our relationship subconsciously early on in their lives.

After the age of six, where memories become more solidified, I continued with appreciable interactions to reinforce our relationship dynamic. This included jogging around the neighborhood while in Kansas, of which Jaleah complained all the time, but participated and completed (begrudgingly). Teaching them how to throw and catch, play basketball as well as go to the park, hike and camp (in the backyard). Beyond that, we did "Daddy-daughter" routine events such as mall visits where we did window shopping and got frozen yogurt or Auntie Annie's pretzels at the mall or afterwards. I note some of these examples because I was cognizant of cost, but I also wanted to spend time at places I believed they would like to go and create other experiences they may not naturally want to do.

I also spent one-on-one time with each daughter. With Jaleah, we played Wii when she was early double-digits every week, followed by weekly walks without any technology when she was in high school. With Jaelin, we had Daddy-daughter talks while Vambie and Jaleah were at gymnastics. These talks covered a variety of topics and were done without distractions (no TV or phones) so she fully appreciated my interest and investment in her ideas and growth.

The most memorable of these experiences was the father-daughter dance we attended while in Kansas. Although it seemed weightier because they were young, upon reflection I do not believe age mattered. They got dressed up; as did I, and it was a formal occasion with food, pomp and circumstance. There was dancing, flowers and pictures, and the evening was all about them. It only happened once; but in my view, it is an event that all fathers should seek out with their daughters.

I also used public forums to express my appreciation and pride. Being in the military, I have had several promotions. Each promotion has a ceremony; and the more senior I got, the more formal and grander the ceremony. In each one, I recognized my family, specifically my mother, wife and daughters. Although not exclusively about them, my last two promotions afforded me the opportunity to publicly speak about how proud I was of them in becoming beautiful young women. I gave them jewelry as tokens of appreciation for them being "my girls." Personally, the physical gifts were secondary to the expression of how proud I was of them.

I made a significant discovery as my family reviewed this book. It underpinned my relationship with both girls during their pre-teen and teenage years, and I did not know about it, although I benefited from it. Vambie had executed a well-crafted plan to foster a strong father-daughter relationship. She sent flowers to the girls after difficult previous days in elementary school but attributed those flowers to me. The girls were very appreciative; and to them, it showed how connected I was with their personal lives and struggles. It caused them to commit to listening to me during my (at times) long and boring lectures. It also set an expectation of male investment that they hold to this day. It proved exceptionally beneficial and goes to the difficulty of pinpointing specific actions or conversations that enable successful children. It also speaks to the "behind the scenes" power one parent can have in strengthening the other's relationship with their children, although keeping it from the other spouse may not be ideal.

I did do some things that similarly resonated with the girls, such as short love notes to them on Valentine's day. Additionally, to offset them having a perception of disproportionate negativity based on our routine talks, I wrote them letters. These letters were generally positive and talked to how proud I was of them as burgeoning young women based on successes academically, athletically and socially. I wrote them every three to five years, not explicitly tied to a single holiday or accomplishment, but just when I felt appropriate. I have included some throughout the book as well, recreated from copies I kept / found. Complementary to my notes and letters, Vambie put notes in their lunches. Collectively, we actively sought to positively express our love and appreciation so that they perceived balance in how we interacted with them throughout their childhood. This was a delicate matter, as sometimes we had to demand more from our girls than they realized they had in them. This demand would lead to us highlighting the bad / shortfalls in situations versus highlighting the good they may have done. We were cognizant of how children can misperceive the ratio of positives and negatives once older, so we invested in balancing this perception early and often. It would also correlate to the importance of building that father-daughter trust. For this I needed mutual openness to allow me to express my views and for them to receive both positives and negatives. This would ultimately best serve them, and it was the foundation both Vambie and I sought during these shaping years.

Mandatory Movie Watching

Mandatory movie watching was something we came up with to expose our girls to cultural references born from generational movies. It enabled different types of conversations, allowed them to appreciate puns and analogies as well as enjoy family time. The movies we selected appealed to either Vambie or me and created long-term enjoyment that thrives into their adulthood.

The girls certainly enjoyed Disney movies and other typical children's movies of their day. However, they did not always have interest in the movies Vambie or I selected. We had established a general set of movies that they would watch, and we ensured we made it work, whether they liked it or not. The timing varied from Friday nights to Saturday mornings, to binge-watching a series over a holiday or spread out over multiple years. They were accompanied by what lessons could be learned or just banter about the characters, the ending or entertainment value. It was not quite as formal as it seems; but over time, Vambie and I knew which series we wanted them to watch, and which individual movies were important to us.

One series was *Star Wars*. As a *Star Wars* fan, and due to the cultural phenomena of the series, this was a no-brainer. However, the fascinating piece was the timing. Because the prequel was coming out, we decided to have them start at Episode I (versus Episode IV to the rest of us). This series was spread over multiple years and culminated with a binge watch of Episodes IV, V and VI over a weekend. The difference in graphics aside, their experience and character appreciation were different than mine; but the iconic music and identification of characters was incorporated into their memory bank.

Another series was *Star Trek*. It is important to realize I am more of a *Star Wars* person, where Vambie is much more of a trekkie. Therefore, we could not do one without the other. Due to the variety of *Star Trek* movies, we were more selective on which we required. The staple, at least for me, was the original *Wrath of Kahn*. We selectively did other ones, including the relaunch *Star Trek* series. In my opinion, if you see the original *Wrath of Kahn* you get what *Star Trek* is all about.

Other series we ensured they watched included *Rocky* (up to *Rocky IV* – my personal favorite), *Indiana Jones, Superman* (the first two with Christopher Reeves), *Aliens, Terminator, The Matrix* and *Lord of the Rings*. In general, we integrated the directed movie watching over about ten years; and it doubled as pure family entertainment as they became teenagers. One of the movies they initially fought being forced to watch was *Indiana Jones*. The first was a Saturday morning watch in our bedroom. They complained about getting up early and watching a movie they were not interested in viewing. As noted earlier, it was not up to them, so eventually we settled into our king-size bed and began to watch. As it turned out, we had to leave before the end, so we stopped early, at which time they complained about not being able to finish. Eventually, we did finish; and we watched about three in that series.

In addition to those series, I had my personal favorites I wanted them to watch. These are not necessarily classics, in fact some can be considered "B" movies; but they resonated with me, so I wanted my girls to watch and experience them as well. This list included *Outsiders, Breakfast Club, Vision Quest* and *Dune*. At a later date, we watched *Enders Game* as in that instance it was a book I enjoyed, had the girls read it, and when the movie came out they were more excited than me to watch it.

The bonding through movies for our family is immeasurable. It further extended to TV shows, and it established an enduring investment and reference within our family. It eventually progressed to a point that Vambie established a standing birthday present of dinner and a movie of her selection. This allowed us to share these series over four to five years (such as *Lord of the Rings*). Because of this, even today, when select songs are played, or references are made to certain movie characters, we have a shared moment that will always exist.

Applying Parental Advice

There have been several occasions where older parents advised me on how they dealt with certain situations that directly applied to my circumstance. Fortunately, I learned how to use that advice when it came to my girls, and the dividend was returned with interest. This section talks to respecting advice from others and tailoring that response to my respective situation. I also talk about using sports as a tool to teach my girls life lessons.

I will start with soccer, but the broader subject is avoiding becoming an overbearing parent who tries harder than their child to excel in a respective sport. It started innocently enough, likely as many children in sporting activities do. Jaelin, who has always been undersized, took to soccer as her sport; and early on, excelled despite her size. She had the energy, drive, determination, speed, quickness and sufficient ball skills to stand out amongst her peers as well as those older and bigger. As a parent who played sports through high school, I knew player development and motivation mattered.

Neither Vambie nor I had any experience in soccer, and we really didn't know what it was before the late 1990s. Therefore, we had to learn the rules and nuances of the sport. After that, it was time to ensure Jaelin could develop and improve, as well as compete, win and represent the family in practice and games. I'd imagine for any parent who either played sports or sees potential in their child who is playing a sport, these are common sentiments.

That is the build-up, and the age reference is around eight-years-old. She initially played recreational soccer, boys and girls; and she progressed to girls travel soccer where, despite playing with older girls, continued to do well. Over time, she emerged as the top player on her team. Unfortunately, that ascension did not yield the same on-field success because players changed teams as they got older; and replacements were not quite as skilled.

As the years passed, the discussion between Vambie and I moved towards practice outside of normal team practice. The belief was that as good as she was, she needed to work harder on her own time to truly reach her potential. The old story of basketball players being on the court practicing without prompting for hours on end comes to mind. Jaelin did not go above and beyond to this level, however; and although she was good, her weaknesses became more prevalent as the competition improved and teams focused on her as a top player. Vambie wanted to get on her—challenge her to do more and if not, voice our disappointment.

It is, at this point, that I held back from that temptation. It was when we were postured to inject ourselves, push her to go outside to practice on her own and demand she more fully commit that I said: "leave it up to her." She had gotten to an age where "soccer drills with Daddy" were no longer advanced enough to get her to the next level, and individual ball skill development was based on her time exclusively.

Why did I argue against "the push?" A co-worker / friend who had a daughter about eight years older than mine had an experience that directly affected my attitude about "pushing" and the potential longer-term consequences. My friend was an avid soccer dad / coach who was highly invested in the game and his daughter's development. His daughter was tall, athletic and very talented. Similarly, he saw the potential and spent time talking, teaching and demanding his daughter go the extra mile, critiqued her play and over time became one of those overbearing parents. He had not realized this and would not have readjusted if his son had not raised the issue to him before his daughter got burnt out. He explained his son told him that if he didn't back off then, she would quit soccer, not because she didn't enjoy it, but due to the pressure and demand from him. As her father, he was sucking the joy from the sport. My friend was taken aback. He was still the loving, caring father who was soft spoken and relatively mild mannered, but clearly the number of conversations with his daughter about soccer and how she performed were overwhelming. To his credit, and my long-term benefit, he talked to his daughter and discovered this was the case. Of note, she was not going to complain, she was simply going to stop playing when the time came. Subsequently she kept playing, earned a partial soccer scholarship to Western Kentucky, that later became a full scholarship, graduated and joined the workforce as an educated, enriched young woman due to her experiences as a student-athlete.

That story resonated with me; although Jaelin was not even a teenager, I saw the path that Vambie or I could easily travel if not careful. So, when Vambie urged me to push Jaelin to practice on her own, I argued that it was on her or she needed to be personally motivated. I also told Vambie the story above, and initially she didn't think it applied, but abided by my recommendation to let it play out.

Eventually Jaelin got accepted into college with a partial soccer scholarship, and I attributed that in part to my friend sharing his story. Therefore, I called and thanked him as it ultimately benefited my daughter.

We demanded our girls play a sport, as well as do an activity. We limited them to one sport and one activity initially, so we would not be overwhelmed ourselves. We did not dictate the sport. As such, one chose soccer, and the other chose gymnastics. I volunteered as a soccer coach and did what many fathers do when their kids are young and playing a sport. Over time, my knowledge of soccer precluded me from coaching, but the opportunity to teach my girls about life through their competitive experiences remained. I used their successes, failures, interpersonal relationships with peers and adults, weaknesses and strengths as the means to reinforce life's lessons. I learned to not focus on the individual accomplishments, but on the lessons that can be taught due to the actions leading up to them.

Each of my girls traveled different paths due to their personalities and their sports, beyond their inherent athletic abilities and work ethic. Therefore, I have very different stories about moments that stand out. Before I get into two particularly noteworthy stories, let me say that each of my girls were exceptional in their own regard. Jaelin was recruited by nearly a dozen quality colleges before her injuries. She earned acclaim in a national soccer tournament and was a force on the soccer field when she put her mind, body and soul into it. Jaleah earned national recognition in gymnastics, including winning the Level 9 Eastern Region Floor Championship; and she was competing as a level 10 (all-around) before her injuries that spanned over two years. Her gymnastic club peers earned four-year athletic scholarships to Big Ten universities, and I truly believe she would have done the same if not for losing two years and never truly attaining full health thereafter.

For the stories, I must first go back to the early years in Jaelin's soccer career. Specifically, after her older teammates had departed. She was of average age, around the age of eight or nine, but she had advanced skills. Obviously, soccer is a team sport, so individual talent only goes so far. For all the years she played in Kansas, her team rarely made it out of pool play in tournaments; despite her best efforts, they never earned a tournament championship. This was particularly impactful because she was the unquestioned best player, so the pressure was squarely on her shoulders. This drought spanned around four years and became very frustrating, to say the least. During one of those disappointing times, I sat down with her and said, "At some point you will win that championship, and though I can't describe the feeling, it will be special," (or something to that effect). It was several years later, and we had since moved to Virginia. After a couple more frustrating tournaments, she eventually earned that first championship trophy and even scored the clinching goal! It was that night that I went into her bedroom to kiss her goodnight that she stopped me before I left and asked,

"Daddy, you remember when you said how I would feel after I won a championship?" I paused, turned around and responded, "Yes." She then looked at me with so much pride and joy and said, "You were right." As she turned back over to go to sleep, I froze for a moment nearly overcome with "papa pride." I then slowly closed the door and smiled as I walked down the hall to my room, with an indescribable joy for my daughter's happiness.

The next story similarly has a special place in my memory. This one involves Jaleah. Her primary sport was gymnastics, an individual sport where what you put in, you get out, and you don't rely on your teammates to determine your success. She had earned many trophies and accolades to reflect that reality. Though both my girls played coach-pitch baseball when they were younger, Jaleah had never experienced the crucible of pressure in team sports. This became obvious when following a soccer game where her sister scored four goals in a 7-6 loss. While Jaelin cried walking off the field, Jaleah asked why she was upset, she scored four goals. Although we tried to explain, she did not understand.

As our girls got older we allowed them to play a second sport. We reduced the stress, cost and expectations significantly, but the opportunity expanded their experiences and enhanced their athleticism. For Jaleah, the sport was softball. We could not find a recreational team for her to play despite our best efforts, so when offered a slot on an elite team, we accepted. As an age reference, she was about eleven-years-old. It had been some years since Jaleah had played softball, and although Jaleah was fast, could catch and throw as well as anyone, she struggled to hit those fast pitches. That is the lead-in to a softball tournament game that pitted two local rivals.

It was a Sunday elimination game, and although we didn't know it was a big game, as the parents started to arrive it was clear from the energy level that this was not just another game. As fate would have it, the other team led by one run going into the bottom of the last inning. Jaleah batted sixth in the lineup. We started the inning with the top of the lineup, and the first three batters all got on base.

The energy (and tension) rose as the fourth batter went up to bat and quickly struck out. Every out upticks the buzz of the exclusively parental crowd. Jaleah creeps to the batter's box and watches the fifth batter also strike out. The energy is now palpable, Jaleah looks to the third base coach and gets the sign. She slowly walks to the plate and stands in the batter box. The next five pitches are a combination of balls and missed swings, eventually getting to three balls and two strikes. Yes, full count, bases loaded, two outs, parents are in a frenzy and all eyes are on Jaleah. She gets the sign again. I shout, "This ain't a spectator sport!" and watch in anticipation. The pitcher winds up, releases the pitch. It is low and out of the strike zone, but Jaleah swings and misses. The game is over. Our team loses, and Jaleah makes the last out.

Now, she trudges off the field back to the truck crying, realizing that she made the last out to end the game. In the front of the truck sat Vambie and I, driving back to our house in Virginia, trying hard to keep our composure … and not laugh out loud. See, this was an excellent lesson and taught her the stark difference between individual and team sports. Also, she succeeded in nearly everything; so, failing in a relatively inconsequential game afforded her a life lesson that words can't capture. I talked to her after she settled down, but there wasn't much consoling that could be done. However, a year later she had improved, played in a lower-level league, earned all-star status, and was in a similar situation with two outs and a runner on third in a tie game. She ended up hitting the game-winning single, but I don't think that made up for the strikeout the year prior.

Disney World Vacation

We had several major trips, some with only the Core 4 and others with extended family. Our family vacation list includes Disneyland Paris (France), Walt Disney World (Florida), Myrtle Beach (South Carolina), a five-day Bahama Cruise and Puerto Rico, to name a few. Each of these vacations have their own story and the girls' ages ranged from under five to over twenty. We have great memories from each, but I will only share one experience—Disney World.

This was the "granddaddy" of our Core 4 trips. We had been to Disneyland Paris while I was stationed in Germany, and there was no doubt Walt Disney World would be added to our list. Also, Vambie nor I had ever been. We planned the Disney trip well in advance, and due to the cost and criteria (more on that later), we had to save for nearly two years to afford it. Vambie and I also set some guidelines leading up to and during the vacation.

First, we decided to wait until each of the girls were at least six. We had seen parents begging little kids to do certain things at parks and we wanted none of that. Also, we wanted them to remember the vacation, and personally believed it would be hazy if done when they were too young. It also gave more time for them to grow and be able to ride all the rides.

Second, we kept it a secret from the girls until we physically arrived at Disney World. We did not want to hear them asking about the trip leading up to it. Additionally, if for some reason it fell through, we didn't want to explain why and deal with all that would come with it. This forced us to be discrete when we talked about Disney, be careful when we planned and make sure our extended family didn't mess up the surprise.

Third was essentially Vambie's edict. "If we are going, we are going all-out. You never know if or when we are going back." This translated to a top-of-the-line hotel, top tier park package and not being cheap on what we really wanted to do. Adhering to her edict, we stayed at the Grand Floridian, got early entry passes to parks, had a suite with two TVs (this was due to a mix up, but we gladly took it) and bought the food package. This was part of the reason it took two years of savings!

Those were the pre-travel conditions. Though our secret was almost compromised, we pulled it off. The last tale we told the girls as we were driving to the park from Georgia was that we were visiting my sister in Florida. Then, the part I know Vambie will never forget. A few minutes away from Universal Studios to watch Cirque du Soleil she turned around and told the girls we were going to Disney. I could not fully see their faces, but think it was more stunned disbelief than excitement. As we rolled into Universal Studios the energy and realization began to emerge.

After the show, and when we got settled in the hotel, I set some ground rules. My ground rules matched my planned approach. I had friends and acquaintances who shared their Disney vacation insights before we went, so I compiled them and built my plan. My approach was to get to the parks we had early entry first, before the lines got long, take a midday break (return to hotel, have a snack / lunch and take a nap), then back out to whatever park was on our itinerary for the rest of the day / night. We did this because staying out late to see fireworks, for example, with a tired and grumpy seven-year-old was not my definition of fun. Because of this approach, I clearly (and a bit forcefully) told the girls that when I said it was time to go, there would be no complaining or "negotiating," it was time to go.

As our first true family vacation where the girls were fully aware of what was going on, I decided to make family announcements to keep everyone on track. One such announcement was that we would not do the Disney Princess breakfast. I can't recall but am pretty certain Vambie and I discussed and agreed to skip the breakfast. But somehow the announcement was not clearly heard or understood. The next morning, when we were going to our early entry park and not the princess breakfast, everyone (including Vambie) gave me side eye (not a term back then, but what I got).

With the schedule begrudgingly set, off we went to the girls' first ever "real" roller coaster ride. The ride was the Rock 'n' Rollercoaster, and it was in no way a kid's ride. We got to the ride and the line was relatively short. As we meander towards the ride there was "vacation tension" amongst the women. They weren't at breakfast with the Disney Princesses, it was wholly my fault and the girls were about to have an experience like none before. Not sure which was most pressing, but the unease was palpable. Since we had recently seen *Lord of the Rings*, I found it appropriate to cite Gandalf's quote about the deep breadth before the exhale. And once again I got the side eye, particularly from the girls.

As we got on the roller coaster, the girls' apprehension increased. But there was no turning around; the seats were there to be sat in. The bar came down, and the roller coaster slowly creeped to its launch point. After a few seconds we were off, and a little over a minute later we were done. In that time the entire tone, tenor and energy shifted. Everyone was smiling, talking about the adrenaline, looking at the picture they took of us during the ride, of which we bought, and just like that our Disney vacation was on!

The plan went as hoped and imagined. We maintained our energy throughout each day, visited the parks, enjoyed our meals, rode the rides and observed fireworks. We truly enjoyed each other and the Disney experience to the fullest. Lastly, to commemorate our time there, we bought the girls Leave a Legacy portraits at Epcot Center before returning home. It was a great vacation and set precedent for future family trips.

Don't Be SAAD (Elementary Edition)

As mentioned in previous sections, my overarching guiding principle with my girls was "don't be SAAD." This translates to proactively avoiding sex, alcohol, abuse and drugs. I introduced this term when they were between eight- and nine-years-old, and I reiterated it at opportune moments throughout high school. Vambie reinforced it with a mother-daughter promise that they not have sex before graduating from high school. It is difficult to trace singular actions as the reason for a given outcome, so the mother-daughter promise may have been more important than my fatherly guiding principles. Regardless of which had the biggest impact, or if both played equal parts, this section covers each part of "don't be SAAD" individually. You will also note the definitions are specific to pre-high school graduation. In a later chapter, I augment the concept for the reality of post-high school living.

S – no Sex: For my girls, this was akin to abstinence. It included all forms of sex as well, meaning no penetration and any "grey" areas that could be argued as "not real sex" by their generation. In our parental talks about relationships, we did not avoid this topic; instead, we incorporated it in routine discussions and reiterated that they should not have sex before graduating high school. Further, this was a pre-double-digit age topic and routinely discussed from an educational, moral and consequence-based perspective through middle and high school. It was important that as a family we were comfortable talking about sex and the ramifications. This "elementary edition" level of discussion enabled more advanced "graduate edition" discussions when they were older and the lines were blurrier. As a father, I did not avoid this subject and leave it for Vambie, or worse their peers / society, to discuss and define with my girls. I accepted the responsibility of providing a male perspective as my inherent duty as a father. This perspective included how boys view girls, the "means to an end" that many boys employ when entering high school relationships and the impact of sex on adolescent relationships. Open and honest discussion early on was our counter to the peer pressure challenges. Reinforced with the no-sex in high school pact between the girls and Vambie, it was paramount that we convinced them to adhere to this tenet.

A – no Alcohol: Drinking, to any extent, was another clearly drawn line not to be crossed before the legal age of twenty-one-years-old. This included legal and consequence-based discussion to reinforce the importance of adhering to this guiding principle. For young girls, drinking can serve as a primer and lead to sex (wanted or unwanted), drugs or abuse. Any combination is catastrophic. Establishing a strong basis for my girls to adopt the legitimacy of no alcohol was critical. In certain respects, it is easier for them to justify consuming "some alcohol" when partying with friends who routinely drink while underage (whether in high school or college). It was a concern that they would accept casual offers due to peer pressure and be compelled to join the crowd, which could eventually lead to an increased comfort with drinking. Vambie and I used real stories of people in compromised situations that may have been raped, abused or publicly humiliated and the extreme difficulty to overcome after the fact. We grouped guarding their drinks from tampering in this topic as others may attempt to put them in a situation without their consent. The balance between allowing more volatile social interaction while precluding complete naiveté regarding how other people partied was admittedly difficult. We assessed each situation individually as we realized once they left the house our ability to control their situations would significantly decrease. This meant our responsibility was to enable exposure to situations where what they believed was challenged by what they saw and pray what we taught caused them to do what is right. Doing this while still in our house allowed for more open discussion about their decisions and how they handled situations, some of which evolved into not keeping the same friends. The no alcohol guiding principle is intended to extend until they turn twenty-one, so we were considerate of this throughout the shaping and teenage years. The balance of how to both educate and expose (in order to reinforce the consequences of not adhering) was not as black and white as the tenet itself, thus active discussion that was open and honest between all of us was key.

A - no Abuse: The types and degree of abuse vary. For this tenet I explained to my girls this included emotional, physical and sexual abuse. With respect to the elementary edition, I explained these three forms of abuse, and I focused on avoidance and intolerance. This is complementary to development of their self-esteem and self-worth. It was important to have established and to sustain a level of trust to enable open and honest discussion on this tenet. As even with ideal relations between parent and children, disclosure of any incident of abuse is difficult to come forth. Realizing the long-term ramifications and difficulty of ever overcoming the psychological effects of abuse, I centered my energy on avoidance. Proactive avoidance, underpinned with absolute intolerance, is what I taught my girls from the start. In the most basic way, even during the single-digit ages, I taught them to immediately leave any man who cheated on them. Intolerance to cheating was a black and white area and not open for negotiation. I acknowledge that when they are older and due to the complex nature of relationships, this could have several alternatives, but I did not want that seed planted in a nine- or ten-year-old girl. I recognize that cheating is not explicitly abuse, but a key countermeasure to abuse avoidance was to enable my girls to have strong self-esteem and high self-worth. As such, I did not want cheating to be perceived as acceptable. This could lead to being with someone who demeans or disrespects them as that would cause a negative self-perception. In relationships where emotional abuse is occurring, the absence of self-esteem contributes to the perpetuation of that situation. Similarly, any man laying a hand on them was deemed intolerable and immediate termination of any association with him was demanded. We reinforced this by the expectation that they tell either me or Vambie. We meant this empowerment to define what is acceptable and not acceptable in any relationship for an inexperienced nine-year-old girl. This also gave tangible reference for not allowing someone to abuse them or take advantage of them. Planting the seed early that I am worth too much to my parents and myself to allow anyone to abuse me physically or cheat on me was the secondary message to this tenet. Finally, we reinforced aggressive avoidance of sexual abuse by use of the "buddy system." This U.S. Army term was used to teach them to not go out alone or be outnumbered by boys in social settings where they can be compromised. It included the reality that sometimes family members are a threat and we consciously considered the environment we put them in relative to their maturity and outlets if a situation may arise. For girls, particularly, we taught them to actively avoid situations where control may be completely lost. This comprised going out with friends who won't leave you behind, forcing siblings to accompany and ensuring each understands they are looking out for the other beforehand. This also included avoiding situations where options were limited and opportunity was extensive. Abuse avoidance may be the most difficult tenet for which to effectively and definitively have countermeasures as the variables are extensive. The primary basis we ultimately employed was investing in raising young women with high self-esteem and self-worth who understood what true friendship meant. This involved carefully identifying who your friends were and determining if they would have your back in difficult situations. It also encompassed recognizing environments where something could get out of control and all the lessons taught up to that point have no bearing on what may transpire. To be honest, of all four "don't be SAAD" areas that concerned me the most, this one was easily at the top.

D - no Drugs: Back to the basics, illegal drug use is a clear, thick line. There is no experimentation with drugs, as any drug use is a big deal; we instilled a mindset that if your friends are doing drugs, that is crossing the line and is a means to no longer associate. This tenet is not bound by age, as the legal ramifications, as well as social and psychological consequences, make avoidance the only consideration for both the elementary and graduate editions. Open discussion about how destructive the use of drugs can be on a person, their aspirations and their family were at the forefront. Although extensive conversation on types of drugs and their affect was not held, the girls attained an appreciation of them through interactions with their peers. Key indicators on whether their friends were involved with drugs included changes in habits, income or how they talked about certain situations. Vambie and I also aggressively queried them if we noticed odd tendencies either with their friends or in their relationships. All of these helped us gauge whether use of drugs or interaction with others who used drugs were present. Not only did we discuss the use of illegal drugs, we also covered addiction to prescription drugs under this tenet. Because we had athletes, and the physical demands introduced prescription drugs, we intermittently explained the potential of addiction to painkillers. We gave examples of how this occurs when recovering from an illness or injury. Our girls generally understood if they have friends who are involved with drugs or are interested in a party that may have drugs, disassociation is the preferred method because guilt by association may generate similar ramifications as active use.

As a father, I held to these tenets throughout my girls' lives. To my understanding, the girls compromised none of these tenets throughout high school. I also acknowledge that parents only know so much, regardless of how attentive we may be. We do not monitor our children 24 / 7, and everyone can mask or hide certain things that occur in their lives from anyone.

Further, I followed these tenets through my high school graduation. Therefore, I was not conflicted when explaining to my girls the merits of adhering to each principle. I recognize some parents have experimented more extensively in their youth; and therefore, may view imposing such constraints as hypocritical. As a peer parent, one thing we try to do for our children is to create the conditions for them to reach their full potential. Exposing our children to the realities we encountered, whether positive or negative, is something we should not avoid. Our poor decisions, whether they proved important to our success or inhibited meeting our full potential, are lessons we should teach to our children.

Explaining the ramifications if you did drink before the legal age or had unprotected sex while in high school can help your children. They may include that information in their decision-making in the hopes of using it to further their goals. This is why we live our lives before our children. Don't avoid such topics for fear they will view you as less of a parent. Honesty versus hypocrisy earns more respect, and although children may not fully realize this, as adults with children of their own, it will become clearer.

As a parent with adult children, I cannot prove a negative anymore then I can directly attribute any singular action to a positive outcome. A complex series of actions and interpretations determine nearly all outcomes in life. I will say, however, our charge as parents is to forthrightly equip our children as best we can based on our experiences and our children's inexperience. Investing in this mantra early and often, with conviction and consistency, is the basis for not only the cumulative effect, but for how I parented during the critical shaping years.

In closing out this chapter, I included the recreated letters each of my girls received following fourth and sixth grade respectively. Due in part to the turbulent transition to Virginia, I wrote each of the girls a letter expressing my pride in how they handled the move and highlighted their successes. I intentionally tried to be positive and encouraging to compensate for what I believed I did less than in our typical verbal conversations.

Jaleah,

This past school year I have seen you mature and develop academically, physically and socially in such ways that make me, as your father, very proud.

Academically: I know it was a tough transition from Kansas to Virginia, and even more difficult going from 'normal' school to a gifted and talented (GT) based school. Although we tried to explain the difference and the impact it could only be understood by doing – which you did, and after the first couple of months you got caught up and was back on top. You continually maintained a high Grade Point Average (GPA) despite those challenges and it shows your mental toughness and resolve to do well, regardless of the situation. You became a lot more patient when we did math, and slowly started to understand that you can read for knowledge, not just to do an assignment or answer a specific question. You made a lot of strides in 4th grade that I am confident you will build upon that and 'take-off' in the 5th.

Physically: You are a natural athlete and no matter what the sport you have the physical gifts to pick it up and eventually excel. But as you know, sports are not just physical – and throughout this year you have grown mentally. As Coach Mindy said, your score improved so much over the course of the year and you got 6th place in states in Level 6 floor after a 3 month break this summer and starting at Level 5! You did as good or better in every event during state and kept a positive attitude throughout. You not only got taller this year, but mentally got stronger. Although we had our fair share of drama, which comes in part with being double digits, you continue to grow. Softball is tough as there is a lot to learn and the pace is tricky (really slow then really fast), but you continue to work and when you do you accomplish noteworthy things (making catches and getting hits). As we talk about in sports life is played out in wins and losses, and you are learning from all these experiences – even (or especially ☺) the painful ones. But much props goes to beating me in that rope climbing competition because you know it is never a 'gimme' when you compete with daddy!

Socially: Moving from Kansas to here was tough; having a sports schedule that takes you out of the neighborhood 4-5 days a week may be tougher. But you are growing, maturing, learning to listen and becoming a social butterfly (maybe still in a cocoon ... but getting there ☺). You are starting to listen and learn, and for me that is very important. I enjoy our conversations on the back porch, and understand we need to get you more 'neighborhood time', but despite the schedule challenges, and the girls at school and on the bus bugging you, you are maturing – and with maturity comes the ability to handle situations better. Once you learn how to handle those situations the real fun begins ... and I look forward to seeing you break out of that cocoon next year!

I love you today, tomorrow and always – no matter what; congratulations on completing 4th grade!

Daddy

The "social butterfly" reference was from *A Bug's Life* as it was one of Jaleah's favorite movies.

Jaelin,

This past school year I have seen you mature and develop academically, physically and socially in such ways that make me, as your father, very proud.

Academically: I remember the early months of 6th grade and every day was both emotionally and academically challenging – where you cried, stressed and felt overwhelmed. But you persevered, did not give up or give in and went from a 3.3 to 3.8 to what will be a 4.0 in the span of 9 months. You have become independent with regard to organization, planning, and executing class requirements and do so very well. I am excited for you going to 7th grade because you have shown so much in the 6th grade.

Physically: My Champion!! You performed beautifully this year in soccer. You not only made the team, but excelled as a great team member that, although not a formal leader, became the top scorer. You listened to Coach Brent and Coach Joe as well as me and mommy and took those comments to the field. You made the most of those opportunities to win and winning that tournament last fall was awesome. Although that may have been a crowning moment, your energy and desire during each of the other tournaments was as impressive. Even getting hurt you showed heart to endure the pain and responded well to your teammates. And I believe the parents and other girls expressed their respect for you as a person, not just an athlete, during that time. Although soccer was the main effort, you also did well in our tennis outings keeping a positive attitude and always trying.

Socially: You not only transitioned to a new area of the country, but had to make all new friends, find a new team and figure out school. Looking back you did it all with a smile (and some drama ☺). You continue to develop keen social skills from generating conversations, injecting humor (though sometimes bad), and having your first boyfriend. You are doing very well in listening to what is said and using that to improve yourself. This year was a big year socially as you had more freedom and experienced different emotions and situations. As you enter middle school, I am confident that what you have learned so far will set you up for success – so don't worry about being stuffed into a locker.

I love you today, tomorrow and always – no matter what; congratulations on completing 6th Grade!

Daddy

The "no matter what" was a *Rocky IV* reference because we had recently watched the Rocky series.

CHAPTER 3
EARLY TEENAGE YEARS

For some, the teenage years may be the most feared phase of upbringing for parents. The generational gap is most obvious during these years; and the differing views on priorities, responsibilities, communication, performance in school / athletics / activities and social norms, to name a few, become more pronounced. The relationship that seemed so strong in the pre-teen years becomes vastly different; and in more extreme situations, the bonds that were not built earlier in the parent-child relationship turn into a thick, black wall with no insights into the thoughts and desires of a seemingly reserved high school student. Further, multiple efforts to bridge these gaps seem to yield minimum tangible improvement; and ultimately, the parents decide to wait it out and hope that what was learned when they were single-digits will produce the desired success at twenty and twenty-one.

The above scenario is a parental perception prior to having kids who are teenagers. Or, it is a reality for some parents when their kids are teenagers, based on talking with other parents with similarly aged kids as mine during that time frame. For *the White House*, the investment during the shaping years and the application of the cumulative effect was a deliberate attempt to offset the worst-case scenario. For me, the beginning of the teenage years was a transition point that dictated a different approach in how we interacted with our girls. The way we talked to them, our expectations on their responses to us and how we defined success were reset relative to their age and maturity. We began to react more to how they perceived the situation as they had opinions, whether voiced or not, whether accurate or illogical, but which needed to be discussed. Otherwise the girls might misinterpret or misapply what we taught early on.

We also shifted our character development focus from self-esteem to self-worth. Though not markedly different, as self-esteem is about confidence and satisfaction in oneself, self-worth is the opinion about yourself and the value you place on yourself. Each are foundational characteristics and ones that I believed were key in enabling my girls to adhere to the "don't be SAAD" tenets. As a father of girls, I decided I could not control the boys, so I had to instill the fortitude in my daughters to combat sex, drugs, alcohol and abuse as teenagers.

As the head of my household, I also worked hard to create a real and perceived safe haven for my girls. Where they were not stressed but could relax, find solitude when necessary, express their feelings without fear and otherwise be at peace in the home and with the core family. It was important that each of us recognized and respected the value of each member individually and collectively. Although interrelations were not always peachy between Vambie and me, she and the girls or the girls and me, there was always a concerted effort to fix the communication breakdown once we determined it was disrupting how we functioned.

Within our core family unit, parental leadership and mentorship correlated to our perceived self-worth. Therefore, Vambie never tempered her input because she knew the value she added. Similarly, for me and my level of engagement, I recognized my girls needed to hear my perspective on any given topic as well.

Every member of our core family had an active role in the maturation and development of the others. We believed that to foster an environment that yields proud and productive children, a perception by the girls that each parent matters and must be respected was vital. For such a perception to exist, each parent had to recognize our self-worth so we could instill it in our girls so they can have it any time they leave the house.

Life Nugget: My Freshmen Year at Georgia –

There are about three central stories from my time as a freshman at college that I parlayed into life nuggets. Because my girls ultimately went to college, I referenced these stories several times after I initially told them, including when they were in college. The first was my father's parting message after dropping me off at the University of Georgia to start my college career. I was over 650 miles away from my home with no family anywhere close. The opportunity for failure when a seventeen-year-old boy is over ten hours from home and on his own for the first time in his life is pretty high. So, my dad gave me some sound guidance that resonated with me early and often in my college career; and I shared the story with my girls. After I was moved into the dorm and right before my dad drove off, he told me my priorities, in case I did not know them. He said, "Priority #1 is education, priority #2 is education and priority #3 is education. Anything after that is up to you." Then he hugged me and left. Whenever I was on the fence about going out or studying, those priorities put me where I should be. The nugget for my girls was understanding what is important and why you are where you are. The second story was about overcoming near failure by trusting in yourself and spending time to address the problem at hand. In this one, I told them about my freshmen English 101 class where I earned a D, an editing failure (a paper with five major grammatical errors was an automatic 20%), another D and a straight F on my first four papers. Within weeks of starting college, I found myself reflecting on my successes that got me to college (generating confidence that I could pass this class) and assessing how I could fix my failures. Fortunately, the teacher allowed rewrites (I believe the highest "new" grade was a C) and after adjusting my writing style I improved enough to earn an overall C. I did not have a lot of Cs my first three years in college, but the one in English 101 was one I was most proud of because of how hard I had to work to earn it. The last specific life nugget derived from my freshmen year was about my third quarter chemistry class. As a chemistry major, I believed if I could not get an A or B in freshmen-level chemistry I may need to reassess my desired degree. This came to a head when I was barely keeping a C in Chemistry 123. The last opportunity to improve was the final exam. I dedicated myself and earned over 100% on the final and with the curve earned an A in the class. I used this story to demonstrate what can be achieved if you fully commit yourself and demand excellence.

Empowering Responsibility

Part of raising a functional independent adult is instilling an attitude of empowerment in young teenagers. To accomplish empowerment, we had to foster independence, personal accountability and responsibility before they left the house. For us, this was the necessary precursor to raising an adult who can live a happy, productive life realizing their full potential for the good of themselves and society. At least that was our premise, and we took actions towards that end.

Empowerment means to give authority to, thereby giving the right to control, judge, or prohibit actions. For some parents, empowerment means high risk, potential for failure and increased likelihood of catastrophic / life-altering decisions where their teenagers can't recover and presumably doom their lives. Sounds a little extreme, but it is likely why helicopter parents exist. Regardless, any of the above are worst case and go to the core of our biggest fears. However, we must achieve a measure of balance if our goal is to have a functional adult after eighteen years of raising a child. At least that is how we viewed it.

This was a tailored process where particular decisions or actions throughout our girls' development transferred the onus from us as parents to them as children. This started before the teenage years with making them responsible for doing certain chores and having a standard to determine if completed. An example was having them wash, dry, fold and put up their clothes at around the age of eight. The approach was holistic and included decisions on participation in sports and activities, to include their criteria for success and commitment. Academically, demanding they do the work while establishing a standard that, if not met, could yield stark consequences. Those consequences included forfeiting participation in sports when we needed to make a point. In one instance when Jaelin was in fifth grade, she had to apologize to the coach and teammates for her failure as a student. In this case, her lack of focus or investment in a science project generated a poor grade. Although we warned her early on that if she did not do what she needed she would not play in the soccer tournament; she either didn't believe us or didn't understand. Either way, her grade reflected her interest (not her competence); and we told her she would not play, but she had to explain why to her team. This put the responsibility squarely on her because the standard was set and her failure to meet it was, to a certain extent, self-imposed. Ultimately, she did play, because the timing allowed her to recover and demonstrate she understood the importance of schoolwork relative to sports. In any scenario, the standard should be reasonable based on the child and situation; and it should be clearly communicated. How the consequences are implemented is equally important to demonstrate the validity of the threat / promise.

From a parenting perspective, our biggest responsibility in the above scenario was defining an acceptable standard and following through with the consequence when the standard was not met. Every parent will have different criteria based on their upbringing, their expectations, their success and failures, and their priorities. Possibly one of the most sensitive topics is what those standards are and how the children interpret them. Every parent must understand the affect and objectively evaluate why and what they allow (and don't allow) their children to do. I included examples of standards we established over the years for our early teenage daughters.

Academics: Vambie would often tell our girls that their job is school. Their top priority upon starting school is to do well and everything else is secondary. This is likely a common belief for many parents, however, the approach to enable success without re-living high school as a parent can vary significantly. We explained to our girls what we expected from them in school, but we did not demand the same level of performance from each. Their unique characteristics affected how much they had to work to achieve their respective grades, and we tempered our scrutiny of them relative to those traits. One child tested as gifted and talented and more easily earned high marks (essentially straight As). The other was smart but had to work harder and her grades would be slightly lower. Each excelled, earning over 3.7 GPAs and taking advanced classes throughout high school, but the dialogue and pressure we applied was different for each child. The summer math / science classes raised their confidence and helped me gauge where they may struggle. This was important in allowing them to find their own way in high school without relying on us. As they got into high school, this translated to them seeking help from teachers, peer students and online before coming to us. As a tactic to empower them, I told my girls to not give me, as a father, credit for their success in school because I didn't want the blame if they did not succeed. There is obviously a degree of credit a proactive parent should receive, but the important point is the child must own their success so they can believe *their* efforts are the critical factor in achieving more.

Athletics / Activities: I played sports when I was in high school. There are also studies that indicate girls who are active in sports perform better in school and socially than those who do not. Therefore, it was a given that our girls would be active in extracurricular activities when they were mentally and physically ready, which equated to about five or six years of age. Early on, we had them identify one sport and one activity. This fluctuated over the years, but due to various reasons, it did not increase significantly throughout high school. Our girls proved exceptional in their respective sports, and it ultimately led to Jaelin receiving a college athletic scholarship to offset the cost of earning an undergraduate degree. Scholarships were not, however, the focal point of their participation in extracurricular activities. In fact, sports were not only a chance to teach life lessons in a unique setting but allowed for empowerment. We consistently told our girls that it was *their* decision to participate in each sport and routinely discussed the purpose of playing that sport. We openly asked if they intended to play sports in college, challenged their level of commitment and tempered sports with their primary job—school. We sought a balance between academic, athletic and social; at times, we sacrificed athletics for this balance. Empowerment required that we not take over and too aggressively impose our goals and aspirations on our girls. This is a natural urge if you see the potential in your child and aspire to offset college costs, but this can burn out a child and be counterproductive. We also sought to publicize their success and introduce them to forums that motivated them to continue high levels of achievement. This included coordinating for an article in the local paper, which involved an interview with the sports writer, so they could tangibly see what success yields. As a side benefit, it allowed us to prepare them for talking about themselves and their experiences to a stranger. It also exposed them to how a fifteen- to twenty-minute interview translated to a half-page newspaper article. For us as parents, remaining objective was the most difficult. We had separate opinions on how good they were, without being defensive, and we had to accept that their talent and work ethic did have a ceiling. Further, once the girls met that threshold, we all had to learn how to accept it and deal with the ramifications. Balance was important, and when the demand dictated compromise, we had to acknowledge those consequences and communicate the associated good and bad. We worked hard to ensure our teenage girls owned this and that they factored in longer-term ramifications (i.e., post-high school / post-college impact) in these discussions and decisions.

Social: Empowerment in the social setting, for this example, is related to money management. For adults and teenagers, this area is inherently challenging; and we typically want more money than we have. As we were a middle then upper middle-class family, the balance between want and need was a daily consideration. We introduced the principles of money management before the teenage years and allowed for multiple years of practical experience that permitted a higher level of discussion and ownership during high school. Talks regarding why something is wanted or needed and other options to reach the same end were important. Sharing cost, even if "ninety to ten" as it helped empower responsibility since they had a portion of the investment. I used this approach when we went to restaurants for a few years. I would always pay for the meal; but since water was free, I left to them to decide if they would use their money for soda, tea, juice or lemonade. This caused them to actively read the menu. Even though drinks were a few dollars, it varied based on the restaurant. It also caused them to pay more attention to the cost of the meals, although that did not necessarily affect what they ordered. Based on how much money they had and / or what they wanted, it was their decision to enjoy a "non-water" beverage at that cost. Interestingly, Jaelin typically went with the free water; Jaleah went with a drink and accepted the cost. After a few years, I reverted to paying the full bill again; and Jaleah wholeheartedly kept getting her drinks (free to her). This was an example; but as often as reasonable, there was some level of teenage involvement in money discussions. Even if the decision was not what they wanted, an explanation of why and other options gave more ownership to our girls when consensus could not be attained. Explaining household finances helped offset the perception we as parents were arbitrarily withholding from the kids. These general discussions helped our girls understand there was no conspiracy to make their lives more difficult. The longer-term benefit of including them in how household money is managed went beyond the short-term reasoning of what to buy and not buy but gave them a reference on how to prioritize their money once they left the house. The goal was to have our teenagers comfortable in handling money and the affairs associated with money when they became adults. Independence in this area was our goal and minimal to no parental management of their adult finances the standard. To achieve this, we consciously involved and educated both girls on money management, and when appropriate treated them more so as a young adult who had a role in how money was spent in the house than as a child who was fully reliant on our decisions as parents.

My Deployment: Serving in the military for over twenty-five years means overseas deployment is inevitable. Fortunately, this was not a common occurrence during my career, unlike some of my peers who endured multiple deployments for twelve to fifteen months at a time. I had a couple, but the one for which I was most aggressive in preparing my girls occurred in 2009-2010 when they were young / pre-teens. It was only a six-month deployment, and as is the case for any military deployment, there was an inherent risk of not returning. It was with this background that I began preparing my girls months before I physically left for life without their father, whether short-term or long-term. I emphasized that all the time we spent up to that point was to prepare them for these types of scenarios. I focused on empowering them, amplifying their self-confidence and making clear my expectation, an expectation that they excel academically and athletically to demonstrate they absorbed the lessons I had been teaching since they were five-years-old. Although I focused on academics and athletics, I anchored the preparation on how they managed their mental and emotional state. I did not want them to regress after so much success each had achieved. Of course, each of the girls dealt with my deployment differently due to their age, their sport and their maturity. Neither dipped academically. Jaleah dealt more with minor injuries that particular season; and although she still did well, her level of success was not as it had been in previous years. I cannot attribute her performance to my deployment, her maturity or the unique demands of her sport; but I do believe my absence played a part. Jaelin actually excelled and earned national recognition, which was the highest honor she ever earned in soccer before, or since my deployment. Similarly, I am not certain to what extent what I said before deployment or what Vambie did while I was deployed enabled her success. The one aspect I cannot directly write of is how Vambie led the household during my absence. She, typical of many military wives, was the interim dad while simultaneously being the full-time mom. Vambie singularly ensured the standards of *the White House* were maintained, if not elevated, because there was no other acceptable option. I know she had mentally, emotionally and spiritually prepared for my deployment as I prepared the girls, and that is another reason why she truly is my help-mate. Eventually I safely returned, and we re-acclimated with each other and reestablished our respective relationships. Relating to our father-daughter relationship, I had explained to the girls beforehand that I had no intention of trying to make up for the time I was gone. Over the six-month deployment I missed certain things that could not be recreated, nor would I try to do more under the auspices that I missed those events. Thus, the transition back was relatively smooth, the family re-defined normal after my return and we reset respective roles. Upon further reflection, each of the girls experienced unique challenges; but I believe they were made stronger because of them.

We commonly grouped and used three of the four above areas (academics, athletics and social) when discussing the girls' strengths and weaknesses as they grew and experienced life. We viewed establishing and communicating standards directly related to empowering responsibility. We also considered prayer and patience as essential to get through many of these high-risk endeavors where the outcome is uncertain because the teenager has such a major role in how it plays out. However, such risk is necessary with a goal of raising a functional adult who can live independently and realize their full potential.

Communication

This was a relationship cornerstone that demanded more from us as parents than our teenage daughters. We established the foundation during the critical shaping years, but our ability to adjust to the teenage dynamic was more important to our long-term relationships. We made this adjustment predicated on some fundamental precepts that dictated why and how we managed these volatile years.

Teens outpace parents in several areas and for multiple reasons. The areas may include how technology factors in day-to-day living, emergence of trends born from their generation and cultural definitions of normal. The reasons include the pace of societal change, the nuances specific to their generation, individual priorities and the naturally sought-after independence. These factors are unique and vast; thus, regardless of how active parents are, we do not naturally fit into the younger generation's world. Herein lies the next challenge we as parents must face: how to enable teenagers to practically realize what we have been teaching when the answers are not black and white?

Once again, there is no handbook that lays out the solutions to this challenge. The variables just touched upon in the previous paragraph don't do justice to the full breadth of human factors multiplied by an equal or greater number of other human factors introduced by their friends, who were influenced by their parents, all of which shaped in a cultural crucible that judges and categorizes people based on gender, sexual orientation, ethnicity, socio-economic standing, and the like. Now, once the teenager enters this environment, we are naturally separated and only partially exposed to the ever changing and dynamic world in which they exist. So, what is a parent to do? I can't speak for everyone else, but for us, there were three factors that drove our approach.

The first facet was communication. Not to be redundant, but communication was both a macro and micro factor, the gateway into where and when we could highlight what we had previously taught. For our girls, the natural coupling with communication was trust—and without trust, we would have struggled to attain any meaningful or actionable information. Communication was not necessarily verbal or initiated by the girls. Body language, academic performance, social interaction with friends, reclusiveness when previously outgoing, these were also forms of communication. But, absent trust, it would have been a one-way conversation that generated conflict by the mere attempt to make it two-way. As most of you probably already know, confrontational conversations don't always achieve what is desired; and rarely is it the way you would like it.

A second factor was actively listening and selectively providing judgmental opinions. We had to simultaneously hear what our teenagers were saying and in a relatively short timeframe, provide insights on how to address. Based on our experience, we have a perspective they don't, but how we engaged in the conversation affected whether we had another meaningful talk in the future. Depending on the subject, we had to determine whether we were advising them (i.e. up to them to decide) or telling them what to do. The potential consequences greatly shaped which was appropriate. To be honest, at this point your individual aptitude and attitude as a parent becomes the shaping factor to both the relationship with the child and the advice given at any of those opportunities.

A third aspect was observing the physical response. Did they actually do something that addressed the issue? Talk could have been extensive, and they could have perceived it as valuable, but in the short-term, if there was no change in behavior then either it was of long-term benefit (meaning we may see the fruit of that conversation years down the road), or of no benefit at all. This required patience with observing change, but we also had to be prepared to change the approach if the same things occurred repeatedly. Again, our aptitude and attitude dictated how we remedied a negative situation. From this, we had to decide if we would allow something to occur two or three times before we changed tactics, or just once. Their behavior also dictated how aggressively we engaged them in conversation, when they were punished, or if we imposed some other consequence. These were all variable based on the situation at hand; at the end of the day, we made decisions that affected us and the girls for many years based on "parent intuitions."

I used some key terms in the above paragraphs such as trust and active listening. Misapplication of tone or a negative attitude, as well as inappropriate disclosure of sensitive information could have undercut the positives gained. At some point, we had to acknowledge that our child was becoming a young adult, and we had to give a certain amount of respect. Trust is a two-way street; just as we wanted them to trust us, they had to see value in offering their trust. Listening to what they said, and not what we thought we heard, influenced that parent-teen trust level. It was also important to listen to what the girls did not say or what topics they chose to avoid. In my view, after you have conversations with your teens, discretely discuss with your spouse or someone in confidence to share your interpretation. However, do not disavow what the teen said, even if it seems stupid, because there was a reason they made those statements. Further, do not publicly announce something that was spoken in private. This is disrespectful, and it will likely negatively affect any future communications. This area can be a struggle because of the perceived sharing of power that a teenager has not earned. A balance must be attained if the abstract lessons taught when they were eight are to be realized when they are sixteen. We managed this sometimes difficult and sensitive subject in various ways, acknowledging each could have undermined any progress made up to this phase of our girls' lives.

Mother-Daughter-Father Relations: This is an example where communication and active listening trumped the tenet of maintaining a unified parental front to our girls. I admit, it is not ideal to talk with a child about their feelings towards the other parent. The consideration is if neither parent is an outlet then the teen may seek someone outside the home who cannot represent the perspective of the parents. When faced with this dilemma, I decided to serve as that outlet and explain how Vambie viewed the situation and sympathize with Jaelin's plight. This was done in the early teen years, but was a bridge until the misunderstandings between the two could be reconciled a few years later. I used the insights to talk with Vambie about Jaelin's perspective while trying to avoid creating a divisive environment which could allow Jaelin to play Vambie against me. I listened to my daughter and gave her options for dealing with the challenge but did not attempt to resolve the problem for her, because it was a mother-daughter challenge that needed to be resolved by those two. I merely served as an outlet for Jaelin and a confidant until ultimate resolution. As a side note, it is important to understand the risk with following this example, as the unified front is held in high regard for many couples and such communications may be offensive. The point to be taken is you, as a parent, must make decisions in real-time that best enable your children to reach their full potential and maintain the integrity of your marriage and family. How that is done may not have an easy answer, but this is an example of what, why and how I made my decision.

Getting around Masking and Deflecting Teenagers: Teenagers learn how adults work either by who they are or what they are exposed to. One trait we as adults adopt is hiding our true feelings, and when someone seeks those out, we deflect them. One could argue, as an adult trait and tactic, this is a good thing to have in certain situations. For teenagers who are exceptionally intelligent and have the personality to manage the potential negative effect on others, it can be done to their satisfaction without perceived consequences. However, one consequence is it allows for the most sensitive aspects of their character to not be exposed and therefore not nurtured and developed. Jaleah had these "masking and deflecting" traits, but allowing them to fester without mature conversation and knowledge on how to reconcile could be damaging later in life. The degree of which can vary based on the child / adult but committing the energy to getting around these barriers is not easy. The examples in this paragraph were a work in progress throughout high school, and we tailored their use to Jaleah. My intent was to create conversations where eventually the more in-depth topics regarding fears, weakness and failures could emerge. Once situations and conversations allowed me to probe for those feelings, I gave my view on how to address, and I invited more discussion on those issues and others that may exists. To do this, we had weekly walks, without technology, to create an environment that was relaxing, routine and comfortable. There was no hidden agenda to get at a certain topic, but it fostered the emergence of those sensitive topics. Any type situation can be created, but the tone is critical because if it becomes offensive, then the teen may completely shut down. Additionally, be prepared to react when opportunities to tangibly discuss topics that may offer solutions to those most sensitive topics arise. An example of an "opportunity" includes when a child gets a poor grade or a confrontation / uncomfortable situation occurs at school or with friends. These are difficult situations, and teens may not welcome these talks, but that should not stop parents from leveraging such opportunities when available. Fostering open and willing communication is an explicit action by the parent in these circumstances, but recognizing the need is as important. Finally, for those with similar challenges, the key parental traits are patience and perseverance. Parents must work these concerns until the child physically leaves the house, otherwise it becomes something others who enter their life at such a personal level will have to address, hopefully successfully. Jaleah still has these attributes but she is also willing to discuss her vulnerabilities with those closest to her.

Non-Idle Threats: As parents, we often threaten our kids in the hope they tighten up before we must follow through. Akin to counting down when warning them to complete a task, we articulate the consequence beforehand; so, they do what we ask for fear it would come to fruition. But there are times when the forewarning does not achieve the desired adherence, and then we must hand down punishment. This played out a couple of times with our girls: once when they were very young, and another when they were early teenagers. Both involved them not doing chores and / or cleaning their rooms. The first instance was during the four- to six-age range and after they demonstrated an inability to clean their play room. Vambie taped up their toys in their toybox and had me take them to the basement. She explained that if they couldn't pick up their toys, then they wouldn't have any. This lasted a week or so, and then they got their toys back. The second instance was when they were in the ten- to twelve-year-range, and it followed a similar pattern. In this instance, both girls were to fold and put up laundry in a timely manner, as well as clean up before bedtime. Clearly, the lesson from earlier did not stick. Though Jaleah had completed her part, Jaelin had not. After due warning, Vambie went upstairs and saw the chores weren't done and the TVs were obviously the problem. Though only Jaelin was at fault, both were blamed for spending too much time watching TV instead of folding clothes, taking their shower and getting ready for bed. As such, Vambie decided she would remove this distraction. We took the TVs out of their rooms that night. In a change from the earlier occurrence, they would not get the TVs back. As it turned out, for reasons beyond just that occasion, the girls would not have TVs in their bedrooms again. The unexpected, but fortuitous, effect (after initial adjustment) was more family TV watching. It also helped diversify their in-home activities and streamline completion of chores. Lastly, it reinforced that if Vambie says she will do something, even if you don't quite believe her, rest assured she will do it.

Differing Perspectives: Strong personalities and individual opinions invariably generate friction and misunderstanding. Although not a common occurrence, we did have drama now and again either in pairs or as an entire group. One such instance occurred when the girls were teenagers, and it was as intense as any we collectively experienced.

It started at the dinner table where I raised questions about house chores and how each viewed the issue. This sparked reactions that spiraled into tears and frustration. At the crux was the accusation from Vambie that the girls were lazy, particularly when it came to cleaning the house. The girls took offense because in their eyes, they diligently worked to keep their rooms clean, do laundry, do the dishes and clean the bathrooms while maintaining good grades and excelling in sports. All three intensely expressed the differing perspectives. The girls expressed how disrespectful it was to say they were lazy. Vambie was adamant they were lazy despite their claims. I was in the middle, recognizing each perspective; but I was unable to effectively resolve the issue. Vambie eventually stormed out and was further upset that I did not back her in the argument. It took nearly a week to reconcile. I came to my own theory about why there were such different views of the same situation. It boiled down to the fundamentally different perspectives of an adult and a child. From a child's perspective, doing something after being reminded "counts" as doing it, and even if not completely done or done well, the attempt also counts towards meeting household responsibilities. Although the girls were mostly responsive, every now and again one wouldn't immediately respond and would have to be reminded. They normally did at least eighty- to ninety-percent of what we expected, like cleaning most of the bathroom but not wiping down the mirror or sweeping the floor. If they missed something, they would go back and finish when told. Thus, in the view of two teenage girls, not only were they doing school work and going to practices, but they were also doing their chores. How could their mother even fix her mouth to say they were lazy, let alone say it often?

The counterpoint also became clear upon further examination. Vambie, not unlike many adults and likely most mothers, does not view attempting as equal to completing. She also did not give them as much credit as they believed they deserved when she had to tell them to do something. In her mind, as teenagers who have lived in her house for over ten years, they should know what needs to be done. She gave the girls no credit if she told them and they didn't immediately do it. If she had to remind them, then at that point they didn't do it at all in her mind. Doing it at that point earned no credit. It just prevented them from getting yelled at. To further her perception of their laziness, there were additional "common area" chores they could do that they wouldn't. For example, our laundry room was not a designated place for them to clean, but they used it and got it dirty. Why would they not clean the room if it was dirty, and why did she need to ask or explain? This is specific to household chores. Vambie coupled this with school shortcomings, such as not completing assignments or not doing well in a class. Grouped together, I understood why she would randomly claim the girls were lazy. Once I could explain the differing perspectives, we all reconciled and moved forward. It was high excitement and unusual drama in *the White House* for those few days, however.

Explaining Unwanted Relocation

As a military servicemember, it was inevitable I would face the dilemma of displacing my girls during a sensitive time of their upbringing. That dilemma occurred during the transition between Jaelin's ninth- and tenth-grade year.

When our girls first started elementary school, Vambie and I made a point to do everything we could to enable each of them to spend at least three years in the same high school. In talking with older parents, we were told that if they can't spend all four years at one high school, try hard to get them three years. This was a little difficult as our girls were two academic years apart, so getting one could compromise the other.

The changing of schools throughout elementary was relatively trivial in comparison to middle and high school. The challenge we faced was the level of academic, social and athletic success our girls achieved while living in the DMV (DC, Maryland, [Northern] Virginia). We lived in the DMV for nearly four years, so Jaelin went from sixth- to ninth-grade, and Jaleah from fourth- to seventh-grade. They both did exceptionally well academically, made good friends in and out of school, and excelled in their respective sports. At the point where we were ready to leave, none in my family, including Vambie, were excited to depart.

To offset this trepidation, we conducted a first ever family discussion on the timing to relocate. The girls were too young to really be involved in previous relocations, and my ability to influence the Army's decision was minimal. But in this circumstance, we were able to involve the girls in what worked best for the family, considering academics, athletics and social factors. To Jaelin's credit, she offered to give up the ideal four-year high school experience to potentially allow Jaleah to get her four years. However, despite discussion and consensus, the family was still seeking ways to stay in the DMV as the reality of physically leaving friends and teammates was more difficult when experienced. Ultimately, we departed for Virginia Beach after Jaelin's ninth-grade year to transition to the new environment. Fortunately, due to my extension, we were able to allow both girls to graduate high school after spending three and four years there respectively.

The conversations were more poignant in the months after arrival particularly for Jaelin because she seemed most unsettled with having to relocate. While in Northern Virginia, she was excelling in soccer on her club team; she was on a regional all-star team who competed nationally. She was also performing exceptionally well in school and making lifelong friends socially. The only negative was her high school soccer experience was frustrating for multiple reasons.

That was the backdrop when I entered her bedroom at our new house in Virginia Beach one evening to talk about "the move." I recognized the frustration she was having in sports and the trepidation of entering a new school after acclimating as a ninth-grader already.

It was important she understood the factors I considered while also feeling empowered now that the move was complete. I explained that as the head of household I had to consider everyone and everything: my profession; each child's academic, athletic and social circumstance in the near, mid and long-term; and the overall lifestyle of all four of us. I spent time detailing why this move was important for me personally and professionally. I outlined the pros and cons relative to her sister's academic and athletic aspirations, particularly the growth opportunity in gymnastics with more near peer teammates. Then I articulated that although her club soccer team in the DMV was probably better than her new team, it was likely her high school team in VAB would be better. I then highlighted the reputation of military children in that they can adapt to new locations. This move provided her the opportunity to exceed the level of success she previously attained, actively learn from the steps she takes, and re-apply those lessons as she progresses through life. I noted that there would be instances throughout her life when she would need to apply these transition lessons, from high school to college, college to the corporate workforce and in various forums personally and professionally thereafter.

It was important to me that she understood the success she was going to attain moving forward re-started at that moment. She needed to work at achieving that success and be accountable for her actions versus blaming the move or using the move as an excuse for what she "would have done if we had not moved." I explained that it was my decision based on my role in this family, and I was responsible for that, but she could only control her attitude and actions, so she needed to focus on having an attitude and taking actions that propelled her forward.

Dealing with Serious Injury

Having children who are athletes introduces the increased likelihood of injury and the associated physical, mental and emotional ramifications that accompany the unfortunate occurrence. We had a string of ACL injuries in our household as Jaelin tore both her ACLs over a three-year period, and Jaleah strained then tore hers over a two-year period (even our dog Ripley tore her LCL during this time). For Jaelin, the consequence was a potential state championship in high school soccer, and a significant reduction in college scholarship offers. She was still able to earn a partial scholarship, however, and play four years with no re-injury.

That was not the scenario for Jaleah, however, as the consequence of her multi-year injury significantly shortened her gymnastics career. The strain that occurred early in the season was initially believed to be a tear warranting surgery. However, while in surgery, it was discovered to not be sufficiently torn to justify actual repair. Therefore, she went through rehabilitation to strengthen her ACL. Once deemed healthy, she started practicing again—but then she had a complete tear. Following successful surgery, she had another setback. She was diagnosed with a fractured back. At this point, Vambie pointed out, "You only have one back." This eventually led to the realization that after her senior year, gymnastics would end.

The impressive part of the story is the mental and emotional journey of a teenager from when the injury initially occurred to the acceptance that her gymnastics career was ending.

Resiliency is something we as parents hope our children attain because in life it will apply at some point. Teaching resiliency is an academic exercise. Experiencing failure or disappointment that tests your mental toughness is not something parents seek because we always want our children to be happy and have success. At the very least, we want to control that environment so they get exposure to failure without seeing it crush them.

After receiving the initial diagnoses, Jaleah was emotionally crushed. For her, gymnastics was her life. For all intents and purposes, all she had known was gymnastics. Since the age of five, she was practicing and competing. She balanced school and social activities against an athletic schedule that demanded three to four hours a day, five to six days a week. She literally did not know what else she would do without gymnastics. I sat at the table with her as she bared her soul to this unfathomable circumstance.

It was after this emotional disclosure that the three-year journey began. At that point, my job as a parent was to nurture and guide her and foster an environment where my child could learn that there is more than gymnastics. Ultimately it would be up to Jaleah to come to grips with her new reality.

I started by reaching out to a friend who had a similar experience when she was young. She had a career-ending injury while in high school. I called her and had Jaleah listen to her plight to let her know there is a light at the end of the tunnel. I cannot say how beneficial that was, but it was my first thought as I attempted to explain that she could now be more active in school activities, hang out with friends and explore interests she did not have time to do before.

There is no substitute for time, and that was a central component in this situation. Over the entire timeframe, Jaleah remained engaged with her gymnastics club and her teammates while spending more time with neighborhood friends and in school activities. Although she still struggled in dealing with the loss of gymnastics, her grades did not falter, and her attitude was still positive. Over the three-year journey the options varied from full return to career ending injury. Jaleah was determined, so she continued to work on getting healthy. We also sought college scholarship opportunities because she was entering the key recruitment timeframe. However, the interest was waning due to her limited participation. This got worse as her teammates were getting offers from top tier colleges and excelling as level 10 gymnasts, but she had to watch and could only imagine.

Eventually, it became clear she would not get any athletic

scholarship offers. At this point, we adjusted focus from excelling to finishing her career without creating long-term health issues. As she entered her senior season, we knew gymnastics would not extend beyond high school graduation.

This recalibration of expectations appeared to be shared amongst all of us. No longer was the score on an apparatus, or how well she performed a routine important. It was about completing routines, remaining committed to what she started over twelve years prior and supporting her teammates. She began teaching younger gymnasts, and they looked up to her. She maintained a positive attitude and balanced pain with stamina. It was remarkable to see. Her career culminated in a typical "Jaleah way" if you will, with a flair that made you perk up, pay attention and marvel. In the second event of her final meet, she slipped off the vault, twisted uncontrollably in the air and landed to an audience of gasps. It looked horrible; after she confirmed she was okay, Jaleah actually did a second vault and landed safely. She then scratched on the uneven bars to ice her neck and at this point we figured she would not complete the competition. But indicative of her drive and commitment to do what she sets her mind to, she mounted the beam and completed her final gymnastics routine as true competitors do—with focus and determination. Most in the audience saw her flail on the vault; many of us knew of her previous injuries, but everyone appreciated her finishing the way she did. After that meet, some of the other gymnasts asked if the coaches would petition for her to compete in regionals, and Jaleah deftly replied "I hope not." It was at that point she knew she had mentally and emotionally moved past gymnastics.

She participated in the final banquet and, as is the club's tradition, gave a parting speech as a graduating senior. This speech was a personal goal because she had seen so many young women before her stand at the podium to capture their years of experiences as gymnasts. She culminated a thirteen-year gymnastics career not the way she wanted (earning spots on the podium in national competitions and competing in college), but in a way she could be proud of nonetheless. Most importantly, several months later after she decided on which college she would attend, and any remnants of furthering her gymnastics career eliminated, she wholeheartedly accepted this truth. She had adjusted her reality, one that excluded gymnastics. She internalized this alternative that only a few years earlier seemed untenable. She maintained gymnastics friendships but expanded her circle of friends beyond what it would have been. She achieved a personal academic goal of attaining a 4.1 GPA and graduating in the top ten percent of her class of over 500 students. She earned academic scholarships for her desired university and by all indications, she moved past gymnastics physically, mentally and emotionally—a feat not always achieved by elite athletes whose careers end prematurely. As a father who saw her initial raw reaction nearly three years prior to the man who saw this strong young woman speak so eloquently to a room full of gymnasts, coaches and parents, I bubbled with pride knowing she had the resiliency to deal with and overcome any challenge life may pose.

School Choice - Real or Imagined

Throughout our girls' teenage years, we balanced the power of involvement and influence with guiding them in the direction that was best in the short and mid-term. It was tricky because you want them to feel like they are affecting the situation, or even making the key decision, but ultimately, you are creating a scenario where the decision is inevitable based on the factors you present. However, there are other times when it is their decision to make and deal with the long-term ramifications. We delicately figured when to apply which approach in two specific instances.

The first instance involved Jaelin during the transition from the DMV to Virginia Beach. She was a rising sophomore and since she took International Baccalaureate (IB) classes her ninth-grade year, she was automatically accepted into the IB program at the host school in Virginia Beach. However, the demand to continue in the IB program would be a significant challenge for her, whether she understood this or not. Both Vambie and I recognized the significance, and we decided choosing the IB program was the least preferred option. As we visited potential high schools to decide where to move, it became a question of which school was the best fit for her. The course load, availability of AP classes and the time requirements with soccer clearly made Kellam the best choice. During this transition, we made a concerted effort to empower her with not only deciding when to leave the DMV but also which schools to consider in VAB. This created the perception that it was her choice, which to a certain extent it was, if she chose correctly.

The art was how to shape the situation so she prioritized the key determinants that would naturally lead to our preferred choice. With that in mind, in our conversations with her we included the strengths and weaknesses of each, the potential conflicts with extracurricular activities, and the flexibility she would attain or lose. All were helpful in guiding her in the direction we felt would be best. Now, this may appear manipulative on the surface—I mean we are talking about an easily influenced fourteen-year-old. I will admit it was somewhat manipulative below the surface as well. Knowing her personality, if she went into the IB program, the stress and strain on her would reverberate throughout the house. Additionally, the benefit of IB versus AP was not appreciable when it came to college entrance standards based on our research at the time. After a few days of discussion and consideration, we were proud when she decided Kellam would be the best choice. We confirmed that was her decision, and we proceeded to enroll her for the upcoming year. Although we shaped the situation, and in certain ways manipulated the conditions, she felt like it was her decision. This helped her transition as she "owned" the school since she selected it. In the longer term, the process improved her confidence in making somewhat difficult decisions. She ultimately excelled academically, athletically and socially in the school she selected, and maybe not obvious at the time, she did get a little help from her loving parents.

A few years later, we were faced with a similar scenario with Jaleah. For her, the lead up was markedly different, and she, ultimately, was the decision-maker. In this scenario, during Jaleah's eighth-grade year she expressed interest in attending one of the Virginia Beach academy schools. Unlike her sister, the timing allowed her to explore the full suite of options the Virginia Beach School District offered. There are nine academies or advanced programs in the district, and respective middle school students can apply to any of them prior to their ninth-grade year. Jaleah let us know which she was interested in attending, however, the one she preferred was not one we thought was best for her. We expressed that when she told us where she wanted to go, the Visual and Performing Arts Academy. This was an unusual choice to us because she was a gymnast and performed already. Additionally, the time demand for a gymnast who is practicing five to six days a week to also meet the Visual and Performing Arts Academy demands seemed like a recipe for disaster during her high school career.

Her mother drove the next set of events. Vambie required she apply to at least four academies / programs if she was applying to the Visual and Performing Arts Academy. Vambie said we could decide after the acceptance results were in. So, Jaleah proceeded to also apply to the IB Program, Mathematics and Science Academy and the Global Studies and World Language Academy. She was accepted into three of the four academies / programs to which she applied. She was not accepted into the IB Program.

Once the testing / application / acceptance process was completed, the discussion about options came next. Based on where we lived and the schools that accepted her, she had four choices when you include Kellam, which was our geographically-aligned high school. The Global Studies and World Language Academy was immediately eliminated after further discussion on their additional requirements. After more discussion about the time requirements and likely conflicts with gymnastics competitions, we convinced her that attending the Visual and Performing Arts Academy was too problematic.

This left our geographic school and the Math and Science Academy. Once we narrowed the options to two, I more aggressively re-engaged. As a scientist, I held the view that each of my girls should get a math or science degree. Although I later recanted that demand, at this point I held that view. Therefore, I pressed Jaleah to choose the Math and Science Academy. I argued it would most challenge her, that she had to demand more of herself and it started with high school. She visited the school and saw other students. Although she loved math, she did not like science. I continued to press and eventually, she decided on what I had recommended.

This is when the story took a turn. Vambie and I continued to discuss the options because it was not obvious to either of us that her decision was the right decision. Two things influenced the redress of her high school choice. First, Vambie has a premise that she doesn't want our kids blaming us for their issues at Thanksgiving dinner "twenty years from now." Secondly, Vambie inevitably has a dream when big decisions need to be made. Vambie woke up one morning saying that she dreamed about it, and the Math and Science Academy was not the place for Jaleah. With those two occurrences, and not being fully convinced myself that I didn't unduly influence her, I sat down with Jaleah a few days later. This time I explained the importance of owning her decision, that she needed to consider all factors, that she will have challenges throughout and Kellam may sufficiently push her to excel as they have AP classes. This was a complete flip from my previous argument. I intentionally and emphatically reset the parameters so that she would not feel beholden to what "Daddy wanted." I needed her to understand this was completely her decision and we, as parents, would support her either way. Ultimately, she decided to forego the Math and Science Academy and go to school with her sister and neighborhood friends. As it turned out, a key determinant was that she often was in a different school than her friends due to her being gifted and talented and, therefore, dislocated. This caused separate sets of friends, namely neighborhood friends, gymnastics friends and school friends, which rarely overlapped. Additionally, she wanted to attend school with her big sister. Separated by two academic years and with her being placed in gifted and talented schools, she missed those opportunities. And to our word, regardless of the reasoning, we supported her decision. She eventually graduated with fond memories from the high school of her choice. To Vambie's point, we have likely avoided hearing about how we "forced her in to the Math and Science Academy" at Thanksgiving dinner "twenty years from now."

As a side note, we discovered officially years later, but which Vambie presumed early on, Jaleah intentionally tanked the IB test to ensure that was not an option. As it turned out, the IB program test was very much like previous IQ tests, and Jaleah decided to take that option off the table by failing the exam.

The transition point between early teenage years and late teenage years is obviously a bit imprecise. I created the demarcation line as late junior / summer prior to senior year in high school. During this timeframe, several things start to come forth. The imminence of high school graduation is palpable, the early / eventual onset of "senioritis" emerges, the unique independence and stress of teenage driving is in full gear, and there is a heightened perception of the teen that they have life figured out. In hindsight we dealt with the late teen years as covered in the following chapter.

My interaction level as a father also shifted to account for the starkly different setting as the only man in the house. I operated with a "divide and conquer" mindset. Living in a house with (pretty much) three women is something that fathers of only daughters fully appreciate. One thing that became obvious when talking to the group was that it was very different than talking to them individually. When the girls were more passive and less opinionated, this was manageable—but with three strong-willed, A-type young (and a little older) women, such group discussions were more difficult (and that is being politically correct). So, I intentionally avoided idle family talk, or as Vambie calls it, their banter. Unless I could dictate the topic and somewhat control the cross-talk, once the women started talking, I passively listened, but I tried my best to not get pulled in. I would do one-on-one talks in separate locations, or when there was only two of us in a given space. That is but one of the many differences in how our family operated during the late teenage years, and it was also a clear indicator that the early teenage years had ended.

CHAPTER 4
LATE TEENAGE YEARS

The latter half of the teenage years yielded significant changes, particularly for the girls. They became seniors in high school, which included getting their driver's licenses and reigning on "top of the totem pole." They subsequently realized their most significant achievement to date: graduating from high school. They then had to make one of their most significant life decisions—what to do after high school. They became what I call "transitional adults" as they departed for college with semi-independence.

In our house, there was no ambiguity. Our girls would be leaving the house after high school; due to our educational level, it was implied that college was the default course of action. We talked about other options, such as seeking technical training locally, working at a low-wage job to save money or even joining the military. Our conversations usually contrasted those options against attending a university. The most certain and direct path to get them out of the house (long-term) and earning enough income to be independent resided in graduating from a four-year university with a degree that set them up for a career of employment.

With clear impending real-life transition coming, we shifted our focus to preparing them for that transition. The shift in focus caused us to be more like advisers, although we clearly maintained final decision authority. Due to the longer-term impact, we did not assume complete control of these critical decisions. It was also the onset of our parent-adult child relationship. During this timeframe, it became clearer that these aren't our "baby girls" anymore, and we needed to not treat them as if they were.

Every year closer to high school graduation amplified the criticality of what we had built during the shaping and early teenage years. This transition became particularly keen from their junior year through the first six to twelve months after high school graduation. It was important that we as parents and them as teenagers were mutually invested in effectively yielding a result that fostered their short to mid-term success. We did not assume they could navigate those waters independently due to the varied associated options and nuances. However, it was not our ultimate decision since they, as future independent adults, had to walk the decided upon path. To the girls' credit, they developed the stamina to listen to and understand the decision factors. We had to have in-depth talks about cost to attend a school, particularly potential student loan debt after graduation; types of degrees and how that affects future employment; geographic considerations with regard to urban, rural, large or medium-size colleges; as well as the varied strengths and weaknesses of the respective universities of interest. We emphasized each aspect that may affect them enjoying their college experience, graduating on schedule, and their debt-to-income ratio once they entered the workforce. Each conversation required them having a vested interest, because both Vambie and I reiterated they weren't coming to live with us after they left the house.

Life Nugget: Gauging Success – *I gave this nugget when they were in college (oldest) and high school (youngest), respectively. It was another whiteboard lesson, and I used it to challenge their understanding of how the workplace assesses success. It had cultural and social relevance because I knew I had two black women entering a corporate environment that typically underpays women (relative to men) and had relatively negative perceptions of black women. The lead in was for them to rate the importance of race/ethnicity, sex/gender, competence and/or communication skills. I asked them to rate the relative importance of each with regard to high school, college and post college (i.e. workplace). This was purely subjective and simply allowed for open discussion on how each aspect was perceived, the uncertainty of knowing whether ethnicity/gender mattered in getting promoted or a pay raise and that people can talk a good game but not know what they are doing. The ratio fluctuated between secondary school and the workplace, and each of them had a different scale based on where they were in life. Lastly, we talked about organizational systems and how they cause these perceptions from either the "top down" or "bottom up." We also discussed how, for most, the perceptions can become their reality. It was a relatively abstract discussion because most of the content was not definitive, but it exposed them to the ambiguities associated with social and cultural interplay with regard to capitalism of which young corporate workers, regardless of gender, should be aware.*

Dreams vs Reality

This can be a sobering conversation to have with your child, particularly if the actions to this point contradict the desires they express. However unpleasant, ensuring our children are aware of their reality is part of our parental responsibility. Fortunately for us, each of our girls put in the work that made available to them more options that wouldn't have been included if they had not committed themselves academically and athletically. Regardless, honesty and objectivity at this point were important. We had to balance optimism and realism because we did not want to discourage the grandest of dreams. At the same time, we were mindful that aspirations without demonstrated performance increase potential risks of failure, and we had to candidly discuss those consequences. This had broad application as it spanned the college they wanted to attend to long-term career and financial goals. For our girls, in the short-term, they wanted to play Division One (D1) sports. Therefore, honest discourse about what was possible and unlikely based on objective information was at the forefront. For sports, there was an easy barometer—what schools actively pursued them and were willing to offer athletic scholarships? Based on that, they had to temper any unrealistic expectations and deal with what was attainable. Although the barometer was not as clear academically, there was a means to gauge expectations as well (I will expand on this later).

Before I get into more details with our girls, I offer this to parents who are or will deal with prospective college students. You must acknowledge the reality of grade point averages, type of classes taken, class ranking, standardized test scores and costs. In addition to athletic and academic factors, you should openly discuss more subjective aspects such as work ethic, social skills and attitude. At that point, both parents and teenagers must be willing to face the reality of what the previous 10+ years have yielded. Acknowledging the reality of past and current situations can contribute to realizing dreams or force the teen to redefine his / her own aspirations. Similarly, a disillusioned parent must be prepared to readjust their expectations and operate in the reality of the circumstances at hand.

Now, back to our specific circumstances. We viewed this crossroad as one of the early steps in the transition to independent adulthood, as well as getting our girls out of the house without them having to come back because there is no other option for them. Based on the types of conversation we had up to this point, all of us had a good idea of what the options were post-high school graduation for each of our girls. We discussed their long-term goals, their strengths and weaknesses, what is required to achieve those goals and what are the short-term objectives to enable achievement of their dreams. I considered these relatively mature topics and required a relationship where both us as parents and them as teens could openly and honestly express our respective opinions. In general, the bigger the dream, the more risk. For the child, they must have a willingness to deal with more extreme consequences. In all instances, we had to establish a common understanding of what sacrifices may be required and the initial steps needed to pursue those ambitions. We did not inhibit them nor try to force them to be a certain way for our own selfish reasons.

Athletics: I will focus on Jaelin in this example since she attended a four-year university on a partial athletic scholarship. Enabling her to play D1 soccer began well before the age of seventeen. After she made the decision to play soccer at five- or six-years-old, we actively engaged in discussion throughout her youth soccer career regarding her goals, the reason she played and her desire to continue year to year. Another consideration was to not burn her out by putting excessive stress on her at too young an age. Once we determined she had the skills and desire to play at the college level, we diligently worked with her, openly talked about her aspirations with respective coaches, and followed the NCAA eligibility process. During her tenth-grade year, she initiated a key action concerning pursuing her dream. We were not versed in all the steps that had to be followed to actually attain a scholarship. Although Vambie and I went to college, it was not for our athletic prowess. Jaelin found a website which helped advertise the aspiring athlete to colleges by distributing videos and building profiles that would resonate with college coaches. Although we ultimately decided not to use this service, it exposed us to the recruiting timeline, the NCAA eligibility process and the proactive efforts we as parents needed to take so coaches knew about Jaelin. This underpinned the team effort that included identifying her criteria for school selection (i.e. style of play, opportunities to play based on upper classmen in her position, geography and number of scholarships potentially available), coaching her in telephonic interviews with interested coaches after official letters of interest were received, and preparing for official and unofficial college visits. We also considered academic factors, particularly the type of degree she wanted to pursue (e.g. International Business) and acceptance criteria. This caused us to further discuss the academic requirements, the different divisions of collegiate athletics (i.e. Division I, II and III) and respective scholarship opportunities (i.e. full, partial, or only financial assistance). These actions were to enable the achievement of mid-term goals, but we included realistic talks about what was likely and unlikely based on her previous accomplishments. The dream vs reality came to a head when she went to a high-level D1 college soccer camp; the coach gave her a candid, but less than flattering, assessment and essentially told her she was not a D1 caliber player for top tier programs such as his. This was sobering for a teen, but it set clear parameters on which schools were viable, and which were not. This contributed to conversations that were more realistic than optimistic, but not discouraging. It also demanded honest scoping of options relative to academic requirements, athletic options and cost considerations. In our case, despite multiple knee injuries, ultimately, she received a partial scholarship offer and accepted it at a prominent university. This helped offset post-graduation costs, and ultimately led to her graduating without student loan debt. It also meant she had a "job" as her participation in soccer was not free. It came with a cost, defined by demand on her time and energy, weekday / weekend travel, practices, stresses of losing or limited playing time, peer-to-peer team relationship strain and coach-player friction. She had to manage all of this in addition to her natural academic workload, personal non-soccer relationships, community volunteering and inherent life / family stress (i.e. Ripley passed during her sophomore soccer season). Over time, we saw a clear change in her perspective. Initially, before physically getting the scholarship and attending school, her priority was soccer, and school was a means to enable her to play at the D1 level. After a few years, school became the priority and soccer was a means to enable her to graduate without debt. Such a change of perspective was a demonstration of her maturity and growth from a teenage girl to a young adult woman.

Academics: Complementary to the athletic discussion, identification of academic options was also an example of how to enable mid-term goals. For our girls, since college was considered the only option, there were routine talks to establish those expectations throughout their life. Therefore, we spent more time talking about which type of university to attend versus the post-high school options noted earlier. We had candid talks about realistic prospects based on GPA, SAT / ACT scores and the types of classes they excelled in. We explicitly discussed cost, to include what amount of financial responsibility we get from them, how much I was willing to pay and the effect of having excessive student loans after graduation. I advised Jaelin that she can dream about any school she wants, whether for athletics or academics, but there will come a time when her prior performance and other constraints will dictate what the real options are. At that time, the hypothetical discussions will end and the practical decisions will begin. The barometer of which universities were viable was partially based on the previous year's freshmen class statistics. Vambie bought a top 500 college book that described the makeup of the various colleges, including what an average incoming freshman looked like the previous year. This was beyond just demographics, but included grade point average, standardized score and high school class standing, among other details. That summation helped us assess not only how difficult it may be for our girls to get accepted—but, as importantly—how competitive they would be for academic scholarships. We knew their numbers, so we could easily gauge where they fell, whether above or below average. If below average, it would be difficult to get in and unlikely to get scholarship money. If above average, it would be easier to get in and more likely to get scholarship offers. Whether we used the book or went online, we researched types of degrees offered, application timelines, school / subject based scholarships available and other relevant information to narrow down the best options for our respective daughter. I will shift to Jaleah at this point because Jaelin was more driven to find a school that offered an athletic scholarship; but at this point, it was pretty clear Jaleah would not get a gymnastic scholarship due to her injuries. As such, we looked at five-year Accounting Masters programs to support her desire to be a Certified Public Account (CPA). We looked at the noted criteria and compared overall costs based on scholarship or cost offsets offered by the respective universities. We had a clear cost consideration based on savings we had; so eventually, it was a discussion on best school for the money. Jaleah knew what was important to her, and based on her personality, we were not constrained by geography. We narrowed it down to two or three and she decided on Eastern Michigan University (EMU). After acceptance, she earned a Resident Assistant (RA) position which further offset costs her scholarship was not covering and ultimately led to having minimum student loan debt despite earning her master's degree. She also earned a semester of college credit from her AP test scores. Like her sister, had paid internships, from which she was able to save money for post-college transition. She has accepted a position at an accounting firm and will have a well-paying job in her field immediately after graduation.

As parents, we are charged to enable our children to reach their full potential. With the experience and the knowledge we have attained, the advice should contribute to reaching that goal. Blindly and ignorantly pushing them into a life they are not equipped to function within makes reaching that potential, and ultimately achieving their dreams, more difficult. Factoring these points in real-time was something we worked hard to do.

College Selection Process

The lead up to enabling our girls to decide on which college to attend began in earnest during Jaelin's tenth-grade year. Because my girls are two academic years apart, it was more blended and began with Jaelin starting the process and ended with Jaleah deciding on where to attend, with no real break in between.

Tangible actions and pragmatic discussion included visiting different types of universities, cost considerations, phone interviews with prospective college coaches, completing applications, recruiting visits and comparing acceptance offers. This lead up was a joint effort, and involved the whole family due to the myriad of factors and allowed for more adult-based conversations.

In addition to a review of academic standing (i.e. classes completed and GPA) and taking standardized tests we imposed an additional requirement: to have them write generic college application essays the summer before the formal process began. Having teenagers and foreseeing the implied challenges associated with time, schedule and energy, I had them draft two to three essays capturing who they are and what their aspirations are agnostic of a specific questionnaire. This would allow them to more easily complete actual application essays and reduce the time and associated stress. This also allowed us to explain the importance of recognizing how accomplished they are and not being shy to articulate.

Another "condition setting" activity was to visit different types of universities to orient my girls and establish criteria for them to use in deciding later. During Spring Break of Jaelin's ninth-grade year, we took a family vacation to Philadelphia primarily to expose our girls to the different types of universities. We visited UPenn, Drexel, St Johns and Temple which exposed them to small, medium and large universities with different missions and settings. This allowed us to talk size, location, types of degrees offered and how each matched their strengths and desires. Further, using the visited schools as a reference, we talked the pros and cons of each, what aspects were important and what factors they would consider in deciding. We also expanded to preferred school size, architecture, student-teacher ratio, school mission, setting (urban vs suburb) as well as the respective "feel" of the universities.

This all dovetailed into the college recruiting and selection process. Although we had to deal with injuries and diminishing offers, we were fully immersed in college recruiting early on. Beginning in September of Jaelin's junior year, the recruiting piece became active because colleges could formally make direct contact with recruits. We had about ten interested schools, so we had to establish criteria to distinguish the options coupled with their academic merits.

One aspect that proved uniquely challenging was the telephone interview with coaches. For soccer, it was important to learn if Jaelin could mesh with the coach, share his views on playing styles, understand their interest in her and articulate what value she had for the program. The difficulty was in Jaelin's discomfort with calling an adult and engaging in a dynamic conversation of this type. I viewed this as a great opportunity to help her learn and refine her communication skills. Jaelin continued to give excuses as to why she could not make the calls; whereby eventually, I had to leave work early to ensure she did what we discussed. Although I could not make the call, I helped with what type of questions to ask, how to introduce herself and pre-scripted answers to potential coach questions. I sat in the room as she made the calls and critiqued how the conversation went afterwards. Once she did about two phone interviews, she became comfortable and was able to complete the remaining calls without me over the next week.

It was soon after that she reinjured her knee—and eventually, the numbers dropped. After rehabilitation and her decision to continue in her D1 sports journey, we reassessed which colleges were viable. This significantly reduced the number of recruiting visits we would take, both officially and unofficially. We ultimately took three unofficial visits, and one official visit. Each visit allowed for father-daughter or mother-daughter time, discussion about what to expect, and post-visit discussion about what went well and what didn't. After we completed all visits, she had two preferred walk-on options and one partial scholarship offer. She decided on the partial scholarship for financial reasons and familiarity with the coach. The maturity of the program was not as strong as the other programs, but the academic opportunities and geographic location made Howard the choice for her.

For Jaleah, the athletic recruiting was even more limited. She had fewer options because her injury occurred earlier in her high school career. The only viable athletic scholarship quickly ended when the gymnastics coach was fired the Sunday before her unofficial visit. Because the assistant coach was not guaranteed to stay on, she could not offer anything to Jaleah. Because that was the singular option, once that fell through, we went exclusively to academic criteria.

Fortunately, Jaleah had more academic scholarship opportunities due to her scholastic accomplishments. Although cost was not initially at the forefront, we eventually tailored her list to those that matched her degree and whose cost was reasonable once we factored in all scholarship offers. We did not visit as many colleges with Jaleah, in part because she did not apply to any schools in Virginia. There were about six schools on her final list. Once we attained all the information, we evaluated them primarily based on business school ranking, five-year accounting degree programs and cost (normalized by tuition / room and board offset by offered scholarships). Geographic location was not a significant factor. The only school she had physically visited was Eastern Michigan, which was her ultimate selection. No other college was significantly better, on paper, than EMU; therefore, as we continued to evaluate, none warranted a visit in Jaleah's view. To what extent that affected her overall selection is not clear. However, after I visited Eastern Michigan and understood their mission, which is to enrich lives in a supportive, intellectually dynamic and diverse community while also preparing students with relevant skills and real-world awareness, I wholeheartedly supported her decision.

For those who have attended college directly from high school, this is commonplace, and I found not that much different from when I experienced it twenty years prior. For those who have not, this process can seem daunting and many facets could be missed, which contributes to changing majors, changing schools, dropping out completely or incurring extreme debt. The sharing of responsibility between each child and us as parents was central to navigating this process. Clearly and realistically setting expectations and parameters was also key. Early and routine discussion about what type of degree to pursue, why that is the option, what job opportunities exist, and how much money that job typically offers complemented college selection. This contributed to each daughter not changing their degree, sustaining scholarships, attaining paid internships, and able to earn an income that enables a livelihood commensurate with being an independent functional adult.

Don't Be SAAD (Graduate Edition)

If throughout your child's development you could not foresee having this type of conversation, whether father to daughter or mother to son, you must honestly assess why not. Parents should determine how often and to what extent we talk about these topics. Only having one spouse talk about these areas is not enough. Different perspectives and genders lend to the breadth of understanding our children will draw from. Mature talks about sex, alcohol, drugs and the respective consequences was commonplace in our house. Otherwise, it would have been left to others to scope and define. I was not comfortable leaving this up to random sources at random times. I was also not willing to feign ignorance and not deal with these areas. Therefore, I used this mantra to be proactive in dealing with the education of my girls.

Active and age appropriate discussion about sex throughout the lives of my girls was important. We not only talked about these topics in sound bites, but also in depth. The conversations were often uncomfortable, but very necessary. For our household, we made a concerted effort to educate our girls and make them comfortable asking questions and discussing topics that may otherwise be avoided. Vambie was more active in discussing sex with our girls than me. Although my conversations were less often, I provided the male view. I explained to them tactics boys use to persuade girls and the general intentions of most boys (i.e. to do whatever they can to convince a girl to sleep with them). This relationship allowed me to be comfortable when I sat down and talked about sex, sexual and physical abuse as well as drugs and alcohol with my girls, who would eventually leave the house with no direct parental oversight.

We also had to be honest about our experiences as well as ignorance concerning things we had or had not dealt with in our lives. I have not experimented with drugs, I did not drink alcohol before twenty-one and I had not been abused. When I talk about these things, I talk from a position of personal ignorance, but I am knowledgeable about how these issues have affected others. There is a balance between raising a naïve and sheltered child versus over-exposing them to high-risk environments that increase the risk for a catastrophic incident. There is risk with each approach, and there is no clear "best practice" to achieve the ideal situation. The extent of exposure any given "sheltered" child faces when they leave the house is variable, and how a young adult will react to that initial exposure is also unknown. How a more experienced child deals with these situations is also variable. These can be scary times, particularly for those of us with girls whose consequences can be more daunting; and a parent's grasp becomes more tenuous. So is the nature of parenthood, and particularly parenting older teenagers.

This graduate version of "don't be SAAD" is more specific and more advanced than the elementary edition. The applicability of this level of discourse was during the later teenage years versus the early teenage years. We had to determine the rate of development of our girls and the timing to have such an in-depth discussion. This is a signature discussion, but not a singular instance about these topic areas. It was more of a culmination of years of dialog and education to proactively prepare them for handling themselves in some of the most sensitive areas in life. Several months before each daughter was scheduled to leave the house for college, I arranged for us to go out to a distinctive restaurant to help leave the desired impression. After establishing why we were there, I ensured the tone left no doubt this was as important a talk as we have ever had. I prepared for this conversation by making notes about what key points I wanted to make, and referenced them during the conversation to ensure I brought them up. After I set the stage, each topic area was specific to pre-and post-twenty-one-year perspectives as this would be the last time I would have such a talk.

S – Sex: My lead in for this subject was that for adults it is not a matter of if, but when and with who. I prefaced that ideally she would wait until marriage, but I acknowledged the likelihood is that she will have sex before marriage. I talked about how relationships change after sex, from both the man and woman's perspective. I explained how the man's view is affected after having sex because it is significantly different from pre-sexual relations. We talked about her experience with physically using / applying condoms because she needs to be versed as much as the man. I explained that not using a condom is never an option until she gets married. I explained the consequences concerning sexually transmitted diseases and unwanted pregnancy. We discussed how pregnancy would be catastrophic relative to her goals and the timing to accomplish some of them. We talked about being clear-minded about her intentions before the heat of the moment as it may cause those intentions (i.e. to protect herself with contraception) to be compromised. Despite her using birth control, using condoms was a must. We also talked about the who, particularly for the first time. We discussed the importance of her choosing who, the reason behind that choice, and the affect that would have on her view of sexual relations in the future. This was a candid and straightforward talk. My intent was to impress upon her that sex is a reality and she must be mature in both having it and dealing with it. I wanted her to understand how it affects relationships from a male perspective. I wanted her to appreciate the potential ramifications if not being disciplined in the preparatory actions (i.e. birth control, condoms, setting, mindset). I reiterated the preference to not have premarital sex, but fully acknowledged that it was unlikely.

The tone of this subject significantly changed in this iteration of the discussion because I knew they were leaving the house as burgeoning adults. Sex is an inevitably for our children, boy or girl, and it is important that we as parents acknowledge this fact. The more important point is the timing of the "graduate-level" conversation on this subject. Studies show that nearly forty percent of high school students have sex before they graduate[1]. Depending on our child, each of us must figure out when to have this talk with our son or daughter. Teenage sex based on ignorance can lead to misinterpretations of values or consequences that create scenarios that may cause future relationship issues. I outlined the relatively advanced conversation I had with my girls, but I believe a similar one is needed for boys. Their understanding of responsibility as they become men is different, but equally important, particularly as sex relates to abuse, alcohol and drugs. The overlap creates what I consider catastrophic events; and although the long-term consequences may be more distinct for girls (i.e. pregnancy, rape, long-term emotional damage), it is very real for boys as well.

I encourage every father to have this type of mature conversation with their daughters and use this section as a guide, if of value. For those with sons, I recommend a similar conversation specific to how women view and react to sexual relations with the mother. The father should initiate the father-son talk early on and continue it throughout his son's teenage years, culminating with a similar type

---

[1] Kann L, McManus T, Harris WA, et al. **Youth Risk Behavior Surveillance — United States, 2017.** MMWR SURVEILL SUMM 2018;67(No. SS-8):1–114

of in-depth talk when appropriate. The timing for these conversations is specific to a given family, but should not be considered from an idealistic perspective, but a realistic one. If you believe your child is in the sixty percent of high school students who are not engaging in sex, then simple talks about not having sex are appropriate. But, if they are not, then you should have the more advanced talk well before this phase. I encourage all parents to be vigilant in discerning which category your teenager fits into so you are not caught reacting to this topic but being proactive.

A – Alcohol: Alcohol consumption was one of the more black and white topic areas. For one, it is illegal to drink before turning twenty-one (period), but number two, it is legal after the age of twenty-one. For my girls, going into college introduced an ease to drink that, absent self-discipline, could happen prior to becoming legal. Mindful that high school students drink at a rate that far exceeds what they are legally allowed (pun intended), I had to establish an accurate baseline because no parent fully knows what their teenager has or has not done. Realism versus idealism once again was at the forefront of this parent-teen conversation. Studies indicate over sixty-five percent of high school students have drank to some extent by the time they graduate[2]. Based on these statistics, do not be ignorant of the indicators of underage drinking. And like sex, if the teen is doing it, handle this conversation based on that reality.

For my girls, alcohol consumption was not an issue. They were relatively sheltered and they decided to not drink and definitely not get drunk. This was the circumstance when we had our graduate "don't be SAAD" talk. For Jaelin, the emphasis was two-fold: one was the impact of drinking as a Division 1 athlete, and second was the vulnerability introduced when a woman gets drunk.

---

[2] Substance Abuse and Mental Health Services Administration. REPORT TO CONGRESS ON THE PREVENTION AND REDUCTION OF UNDERAGE DRINKINGExternal. Rockville, MD: U.S. Department of Health and Human Services; 2017

Because of the relatively sheltered upbringing, I spent time explaining the consequences of drinking relative to her athletic scholarship. Then we discussed the risk of getting drunk at parties, once able to drink, because she could lose consciousness or otherwise be vulnerable to abuse. The ramifications of alcoholism are extensive, and it offers opportunities for some bad things to happen. I did not have personal experience with underage drinking or alcoholism; and because this was not an issue with my girls, I provided limited examples of these consequences. It was not difficult to impress upon them the importance of avoidance until twenty-one, and once legal, we further discussed moderation and control to ensure alcohol remains a social beverage only.

A – (No) Abuse: In my opinion, abuse is the most complex of the topic areas. The effect on a child who experiences emotional, physical and / or sexual abuse can be extensive and may never be completely overcome. The other areas could be considered self-inflicted due to ignorance, but abuse can be imposed by someone else due to variables not as easily controlled. Further, failure to proactively avoid any type of abuse creates an experience that is difficult to overcome and introduces an obstacle to truly realizing happiness and joy that parents desire for their children.

As our children leave what was a safe and loving household, the vulnerability to being involved in a relationship that could be emotionally or physically abusive increases. Over-aggressive parenting, where parents seek extreme control, may make the child more susceptible to being involved in such destructive relationships once that oversight is removed. Children who are not educated to recognize situations that increase their vulnerability, or who have habits that amplify the potential to be abused, become more likely candidates for negative life-altering experiences. This topic area has the scary potential to couple with any, or every, other aspect within the canopy of "don't be SAAD." We made special emphasis to impress upon our girls that aggressive proactive actions are needed to avoid the long-term effects associated with being a victim of abuse. Similarly, we impressed upon them the cumulative effect of building self-esteem and self-respect to create intolerance for such behavior from others at a young age—and we reinforced the concept throughout their upbringing.

The previous paragraph describes my premise and dictates the tactic I used to prevent abuse, but it is difficult to prove a negative. My girls were not abused, and we made a conscious effort to not put them in situations where they could be abused. This was the baseline we established before they physically left the house and was the starting point for equipping them to avoid similar situations when parental oversight was removed.

I focused the graduate-level conversation on the importance of proactively avoiding settings that are conducive for abuse, recognizing situations that may cause them to be susceptible and acceptable reactions if faced with the potential of any abuse. I reinforced not drinking before the legal age, and not getting drunk even when of legal age because it could put them in a vulnerable position. Identifying indicators while in relationships and addressing them before they manifest into abusive actions was also important. Further, I gave a personal example where, despite all the above, I was in an otherwise vulnerable position and it was decisive and aggressive action on my part that prevented anything from happening and allowed a painless resolution. But most importantly for my girls, I told them to take a mindset that a potentially abusive situation is a life or death situation. They need to have a mindset that their very life is in danger and take any action necessary to preserve themselves even at the cost of the abuser's life / well-being. I would rather deal with those consequences than a "he said, she said" where a perception of consent is perpetrated. This is an extreme point; but as a father who has heard of too many instances where girls are sexually abused without punishment to the abuser, I refused to not empower my girls if they are, God forbid, faced with such a situation. For me personally, that is a life or death situation; and I made a point to impress this on my girls. Further, for all fathers, I invite you to do the same with your daughters.

D – (No) Drugs: As with abuse, "no" remains in front of this topic area. For illegal drugs, there is no point in life where the use of drugs is acceptable. This is as simple as any of the four areas and did not require a lot of elaboration during our signature discussion. We did not differentiate between the various types of drugs, although we did talk about the use of prescription drugs to ensure they didn't get addicted. For us, single use of illegal drugs opens the door that sometimes cannot be closed without much pain, if not a catastrophic ending. Because of the relatively sheltered life of our girls and active discussion about the physical and legal consequences of illegal drug use, the explanation of the ramifications was short and simple.

An area we did spend some time on was association with those who do use drugs. Destructive habits of friends is not always clear early on in relationships, but how you respond once you discover negative habits becomes a decision point. Not deciding to terminate any destructive relationship is a decision in and of itself. A point of emphasis was to disassociate themselves from individuals who do engage in drug use. Guilt by association is a reality in circumstances where drugs are involved. The habits typically linked to drug users are not conducive to achieving the goals we aspire our girls to have. It should be noted that I did not provide similar advice regarding underage drinking. Drugs and alcohol are different, and the talking points of each were notably different.

Regarding both the elementary and graduate editions of "don't be SAAD," the reasoning behind this basic parental approach is to avoid a catastrophic incident before adulthood. For my family, a catastrophic event would be commitment / conviction of a crime, pregnancy, sexual abuse / rape, drug addiction or alcoholism. Any of these type experiences may drastically affect their ability to realize mid-term goals and could affect longer-term goals. Communication early and often on what they should not do as a "left and right limit" was central. We also actively engaged in age appropriate conversations about such topics as peer pressure, friends' habits and relationships. These conversations allowed us to recognize the mindset of our girls. We have been blessed that this approach yielded the desired results, and certainly this is just one way of achieving such an end. The more important takeaway is to have an approach and implement that plan consistently and with conviction.

For those with sons, you will have to tailor some aspects to be gender appropriate. I did not give specific examples, but sex and abuse would be unique to boys in some instances. However, alcohol and drugs would be gender agnostic. Fathers should recognize their role in talking about sex and relationships with their daughters. Mothers should not be the only source to their girls regarding what men seek and expect in relationships. The maturity difference is commonly recognized between boys and girls—and as such, you should tailor the timing of these types of conversations to the gender and environment the teenager is immersed within.

Reinforcing Life Skills

The last formal phase in preparing our girls to become independent adults was tying many of the lessons we taught since the age of six with life experiences from a decade of living. A key factor for the final transition was the ability for us to have mature and realistic conversations with our teens. The presence of a foundation established over the previous ten to twelve years determined the tone of these conversations and how much compensatory work was needed to get them where we believed they should be. We tailored the skills to be reinforced to the girls. Topic areas included personal and professional life balance, money management and defining success. Obviously, the span of topics can vary. The three noted were of keen interest to me, so I made a concerted effort to reinforce them now that they were closer to actually experiencing them. In general, I believe each parent's views on life will dictate which topics they highlight as this final transition to independent adulthood is reached.

As parents who have realized success and failure, we should be able to share those experiences with our children. The timing of when to discuss should be based on when they are expected to become fully independent. In my view, college is a transition to adulthood that allows for some of these areas to be introduced before college graduation or deferred until after. If adopting a two-level approach, then this list has been in the works in some form since high school. If only a one-level was attainable and your child is going to college, then during the college years those areas become more prominent during the last couple of years of college. A goal is to have each of the noted areas fully managed and understood when they are autonomous, or as soon as possible thereafter.

Each noted area can have a chapter for itself, and some of the conversations I had with the girls were fairly extensive and far reaching, particularly for defining success. I summarize a few in this chapter, but I will not cover each one. For you, your life and experiences will certainly allow you to discuss the benefits and ramifications of not doing / understanding any given aspect. I provide a couple of examples of how I addressed a given subject with my girls.

Money Management: From my experience, understanding the practical definition of money management is a critical life skill. Therefore, at an early age we started the comprehensive process of educating our girls both practically and in conversation about managing money. It started in earnest when they were around ten-years-old with them making my lunch and receiving an hourly wage. This was my practical way of teaching them the difference between hourly and salary wages. Complementary to the practice was the explanation about the differences between working in fast food restaurants to government employment to corporate-type jobs. Each included the pros, cons and reasons to pursue any given field whether a short-term job, less pay for more stability or more risk but more money. Having my kids make my lunch allowed for other lessons to be taught besides money, although that was the primary reason. Over the seven to eight years they made my lunch, we systematically taught the various ways to access money. Early on, it was cash or homemade checks (to replicate real checks). Then we created child accounts with debit cards whose balance required management. Eventually I added them to my credit card and I explained how to manage various sources of money while overseeing how they spent their money. As I presented these various forms of accessing money, I explained cash flow, aggregated income, savings versus checking, credit card interest rates and debt management. One of the last examples to illustrate overall money management was walking each daughter through our budget. I set up an excel spreadsheet with all the monthly bills, discretionary money and various allocations to loans and credit cards. We sat down at the computer, and I walked each of them through how much money goes where and why. This included the ratio of car payments to mortgage to insurance to each respective utility bill in order to demonstrate the importance of holistically considering want versus need and what the ramifications are. Additionally, I explained how the income to debt ratio affected my credit score. This allowed for a more in-depth explanation of the impact of a bad credit score on getting loans and low interest rates for things such as car loans. The cumulative effect of these conversations and "jobs" introduced the complexity of money management that without such examples could be assumed simple when in reality, is not nearly so. Intermittently through college, once they had their own credit card to help build their credit score, we would have conversations about managing credit card balance, understanding interest rates, and we could more tangibly talk about priorities, setting aside money to pay on or pay off bills and importance of allocating funds. As a side, I explained the importance of married couples discussing who is best suited to manage family finances and, once decided upon, that each individual accepts their role and functions accordingly. The last statement was to provide a reference for conversations later in life. But in general, we predicated the reinforcement on years of active financial education that culminated with them having an innate appreciation of what it means to manage income, regardless of how much.

College / Professional Transition: In preparation for the transition to college, we talked about commitment, discipline and work levels necessary to ensure the girls didn't become part of the roughly forty percent of first time undergraduates who don't graduate within six years. The transition from living at home to assuming near full responsibility in a distant university is very difficult to replicate. Active discussion about college started in earnest in ninth- and tenth-grade with opportunity talks in middle school (two levels up). With both my girls, we talked about their decisions and actions regarding responsibilities and accountability. I paid attention when they demonstrated immaturity during their senior year as a reference that allowed examples of what not to do in college. Conversations centered on specific situations that may arise in areas of education, time management and social dynamics in a college setting. Because I went to college directly out of high school, I could leverage my personal experience in giving examples of how to overcome challenges and deal with unique circumstances. One of the tenets I expressed was that you cannot graduate from college in one year. Therefore, don't try to attend every party because you have three more years to attend "the party of the year." Don't try to do everything school has to offer in your first year because the learning curve is steep after your freshmen year, but you need to get through the first year to understand that without consequence. I also talked about how life changes when you graduate from college and become a professional who is fully independent. This led to conversations about owning a car, renting an apartment, managing your time / priorities, and all the responsibilities that come when you are an independent adult. Following the one-level up principle, we talked about early to mid-grade professionals in a corporate workplace, since both were seeking business degrees. I was grooming each to eventually become corporate executives, so communication with seniors and peers, leadership tenets, grasping and solving complex problems, appreciating the perspective of organizational leaders were all tied into our talks during holiday breaks. I made a deliberate effort to reinforce work-life challenges to ensure they understood the mindset needed to practically apply what they had been taught as adults.

Own Your Space: This was a life nugget unexpectedly brought about after Jaelin experienced something that unless lived could not be truly explained by a parent. She spent a weekend at a male friend's house in a very affluent neighborhood in North Carolina. It is what I consider "old southern money" as the group she hung around with that weekend were predominantly white and rich. However, her friend was black and his father was affluent. He grew up in that neighborhood, and he was known by everyone—

peers and adults. She took this trip during a college break. It was an extended weekend and she was exposed to a part of society a military, middle / upper middle-class black girl simply does not see. It was the last night, and there was an evening event that included maids and servants (all who were black) with as expected food and drinks but, less expectedly, drugs. The setting is as you would see on TV depicting the upper echelon of white society, but perhaps would not believe as most of us don't get exposed to it in real life. Well, Jaelin was in it, but she was not known and was black, so the way people reacted to her was not natural, at least to Jaelin. The adults were inquisitive to see a new "black" face, as only her friend was known to them, and some assumed she was part of the help staff. Her peers, friends of her male friend, had adjusted to her being around by that point. The maids and servants were curious because they knew she was not part of the help staff, but they did not know how she got to this party. All of it was overwhelming for Jaelin. She could not comprehend the social pecking order, took offense to being considered part of the help staff and saw how easy it was to get and use drugs. She adjusted, regardless of how uncomfortable she felt, and she made it through the night and the trip overall. It was when we picked her up that she voiced her confusion, disbelief and discomfort. We could only listen, she was not ready to hear our explanation of that segment of society yet. It was a few days later that I leveraged that experience as a life nugget. I explained how different parts of the country and segments of society function and how, for them, normal is different than other segments. I also taught the most important lesson that she should not feel awkward or out of place at any time. I explained that wherever she is, is where she is supposed to be. She earned the right by who she is, my daughter, or what she achieved. I reinforced that sentiment spiritually by explaining that God put her there (wherever there is), and she needs to own it and not allow anyone to question her presence. It served as a confidence message for an emerging young adult who needed clarity between entitlement and empowerment. If she earned it or deserved it, it is not entitlement. She should feel empowered to be who she is and exist in the space God had set for her, whether with affluent people or less fortunate. As a minority my entire life and in my career, owning my space and being confident that I earned the right to exist beside whomever is standing next to me was / is a critical life skill. Additionally, specific for her future corporate career, potentially being the only black female seeking to excel in any given job / setting, she cannot spend time wondering if she belongs. If she is pondering that question then she is not spending time reading the room, rehearsing her talking points or deftly answering questions posed. That creates a disadvantage that may be subtle but could negatively distinguish her from her peers who do not share such trepidation or concern. It was a lesson I did not expect to teach, but an opportunity I felt had to be taken advantage of.

As I have mentioned before, in my view college students are "transitional adults" because they don't have full autonomy or responsibility. There is a level of reliance in several aspects of living but they also are independent in many respects that put parents in more of an advisory position. This creates a relationship between emerging adults and parents that is unlike the high school relationship or when they are fully autonomous. For my family, Vambie and the girls developed a routine in communicating, sharing views and building their relationship as adult women. My girls and I did not communicate at the same rate. It was more intermittent and based on specific situations, coupled with weekly texts to assist with the transition to actual adulthood. I coupled these texts with calls, visits and shared time during family get togethers. I provided prayers, scripture and life lessons on leadership, success and happiness to build upon what we taught in their youth that they could reference then or in the future.

Similarly, we factored how to prepare for what happens after college into the type of degree chosen and longer-term goals. We talked about how promotion systems work, and how young professionals are assessed during their tenure. Additionally, we exposed them to different work environments and introduced them to others who have experience in the field they want to pursue. More importantly, the level of conversation was mature and commensurate with the level of responsibility they were embarking upon. The type and level of discussion reflected the preparedness of both us as parents and them as emerging adults to transition to this new phase of their life.

Possibly one of the most important things for the family to appreciate during the transition is who is responsible for what. When teenagers are on the precipice of high school graduation and the reality of imminent adulthood becomes apparent, parents should be available to offer honesty and clarity on what must be done. However, parental advice is only part of the responsibility and although important, true ownership resides with the teenager. The teenager is responsible for deciding and committing themselves to that decision. The parent should not attempt to take ownership, but should advise on the associated realistic pros and cons. The teenager must take actions to demonstrate investment in achieving their short or mid-term goals. We have to encourage them and set benchmarks to reinforce the consequences of not completing needed actions. During this time, parents will either set or reinforce conditions for their children to become independent and functional or dependent and potentially dysfunctional. Absent active parental involvement, the situation will play out and may not work out in either the child or the parents' favor during this transition period.

As a pre-cursor, each parent needs to agree on what they are trying to enable, and the teenager must express candidly what they desire. If they want to leave the house, but they fear failure or are uncertain how to be an autonomous adult, put that on the table and openly address. Set a timeline and goals that better align the respective goals so that practical actions can be measured and pursued to a common end. Avoidance and assumptions are not solutions and do not foster a healthy realization of what adulthood is. If you as a parent don't accept that "in-home" parenting of your children has a shelf life, then your parenting approach up to this point likely has been shaped in a way that reflects that fact.

In closing this chapter, and this portion of the book that captures the development and implementation of a parenting philosophy that spanned nearly twenty years, below are the letters I sent to my girls as they matriculated through college and turned or neared twenty-one years of age. I genuinely saw the traits that I sought to instill when they were five-years-old, and I felt both pride in their growth and gratification in how we contributed to their development as beautiful young women.

Jaleah,

It has been a bit since I sent you this type of letter, and regardless of how often I may or may not tell you, I want you to know (beyond a doubt) that I am so proud of you and how you are developing as a young woman.

Your maturity is already impressive as you finished strong in high school, achieving your goal of a 4.0, masterfully managed the end of your gymnastics career, achieved Dean's List in your first year of college that happened to be nearly a thousand miles away, earned an RA job, and did so well at your internship that they offered you two more years! You have smoothly handled this transition in life and immersion in a setting with new people as well as a different culture. You exceeded expectations in how you dealt with the variability that goes with moving out of state and living away from home.

You continue to develop the attributes that will allow you to achieve your goals. You acclimated well to college life – academically and socially; you are mindful of short and mid-term goals, and already setting the path to achieving both; you have a positive attitude about building and maintaining friendships and you are sustaining a strong bond with family, particularly your mother and sister.

I see your spiritual, emotional and mental growth from month to month, and know that despite the clear outward confidence, inwardly you are humble, dogged in ensuring you can perform to your standards, and caring of those closest to you. You are my heart, the youngest who demands so much of herself and those around her, but unconditionally loves her family and friends. Your beauty inside and out continues to grow as does my pride when I get to laud your achievements to others.

I love you, I am proud of you, and it humbles me that you are my daughter.

Your Father,
Dad

Jaelin,

It has been a few years since I sent you this type of letter, and regardless of how often I may or may not tell you, I want you to know (beyond a doubt) that I am so proud of you and how you are developing as a young woman.

As you are nearing the end of your college tenure, you have once again established yourself as someone who has drive, determination and resilience. You have endured the difficulties of Howard Soccer, but maintained an attitude and energy that has not precluded the team's success. You are effectively managing your time to allow for academic growth, relationship building with friends and your boyfriend as well as visiting and spending time with family.

I see a young woman who is arcing towards realizing her mid-term potential. You are having moderate academic success which is allowing you to achieve short-term goals (i.e. internships and graduating); your temperament with building friendships is impressive amidst all your other priorities; your maturity in your relationship with your boyfriend is healthy; and your ability to maintain a strong bond with family (particularly your mother and sister) is also something that I am happy with as that tie is not inherent in all families.

You are establishing the characteristics that I as a father prayed you would start to pick up at this point in your life – work ethic, demand for excellence but the resilience to respond to setbacks and reset goals; relationship standards; balance in how you live and manage your life; and an overall mindset that aligns with the best that me as a father would want for his oldest daughter.

You are my soul, I see so much of me in you and our personalities naturally align. Your success resonates with me so much, and every milestone you reach is reflective of our investment in you as a future adult. Your beauty inside and out continues to grow.

I love you, I am proud of you, and it humbles me that you are my daughter.

Your Father,
Daddy

CHAPTER 5
PREPARING FOR EMPTY NEST

As a parent, I would not say there is ever an end game, but there are certainly transition points whereby the parent-child relationship noticeably changes. These changes are recognizable during the teenage years, particularly when they start driving, but most prominently during the post-high school years and when we as parents eventually become "empty nesters." For Vambie and I, we knew our girls would eventually graduate high school and leave the house, presumably for college. This was a known point, traced back to when the girls started kindergarten. It was not something that surprised us, although it was hard to fully appreciate when they were six-years-old. When the light came closer, and the realization of imminent change emerged, condition and expectation setting once again applied.

Prior to Jaelin leaving for college, I started to create new traditions to help ease the turbulence that I knew would accompany her departing. Throughout the girls' lives, Vambie and I made a concerted effort to establish routines and reliable references for them. These references made establishing new traditions easier as the kids understood the value of such routines. As much as reasonable we blended the old with the new, maintaining what we already did and replacing what no longer applied. Therefore, before I explain what new traditions were created tailored towards being empty nesters, I will share some of those we did when the girls were still in the house.

Family Traditions

All of our traditions were not tied to school, chores or couched under the pretext of raising functional adults. We also incorporated fun and games into our routines which had no critical life lessons to be taught or underlying messages that needed to be conveyed. These traditions, such as game night, broke up the relatively high stress "rat race" associated with excelling in school and sports. It was intended for the Core 4 to spend time with each other, generate memories and to laugh. It also allowed the girls to be more comfortable around us, see that we have personalities and have a tangible reference about having fun with mom and dad.

Relative to games and fun, I need to shed some light on some family characteristics that I have not fully explained to this point. First, I want to state upfront that I believe I am fairly self-aware and know what things I do well. Second, I believe I know what my strongest attributes are not. With that said, I recognize that if family or friends were asked to do word association, they would not associate emotional or fun with me. However, many would say that I am funny, at least those who really know me. And being funny is additive when talking fun and games in my book. Also, in my defense, I do have a soft side, just most people don't see it.

On the other hand, universally you'll hear how much people enjoy being around Vambie and how much fun they have spending time with her. This is born from her personality, her genuineness, and her comfort with saying what most are thinking in her naturally disarming way. To appreciate that combination, remember that she was not only voted class clown, but also vice president of her senior class in high school. Coupled with her willingness to do fun things, people truly enjoy their time with her, me included. In short (no pun intended), she creates an energy by her presence, and if you were not having fun before she arrived, you certainly would after.

This contrast in character traits, and factoring the girls' inherent

113

combination of those traits, created a certain family dynamic. I will admit, when we have fun as a family, I am not necessarily the person who generates the energy. However, since I am funny and relatively quick-witted, I contribute in different ways. Also, there is a competitive streak in all four of us. Since we all played sports in some form, each has a level of investment in any game or activity. Mindful, that "streak" exists more in some than others, and I will leave it at that.

Day / Nights Out: A staple routine of ours were dinners out as a family. This varied from weekly to monthly, based on discretionary income, and included special occasions. These dinners allowed us to change things up, experience new restaurants and have conversations outside the normal setting.

We did other local family outings such as bowling and golf as well. The golf routine was exclusively done when the girls were fairly young, between four- and nine-years-old. During that time frame it was a weekly event. Typically, we played on Sunday evenings as both Vambie and I were avid golfers back then and this allowed us to enjoy a hobby under the auspices of family time. As members of the military installation golf course, they allowed us to take the girls out in our respective carts. We typically played nine holes, which would take less than two hours, and we made sure the girls had their drinks, snacks and maybe something to read. At times we would allow them to join us on the putting green to hold the flag, for example, as their excitement waned after a few holes. Just as a reminder, smartphones were not a thing back then, so alternative entertainment options were limited. This particular routine tended to be more fun for me and Vambie than the girls, but there certainly are memories.

The most prominent of the memories involved the carts and the girls, not any particular shot during a round of golf. Any time we played, one of the girls rode with me and the other with Vambie. In between holes they sat in their respective passenger seat and did what they were doing—eating, drinking or just riding along. In one instance, as we were looking for a ball, a quick decision was made to change direction. So, the driver, not to name names, took a sharp turn at a relatively high cart speed and without the respective daughter fully paying attention, yes, said little girl went flying out of the cart onto the fairway. After a few tears, some consoling and confirmation she was okay, the other cart riders and the culprit parent laughed, a lot. And when it happened again a few months later to the other daughter, similar checks were made, and similar laughter followed, as well as years of smiles and chuckles upon reflection.

The blending of old and new routines is reflective in Vambie's birthday dinner and movie. This routine, which began before the girls left the house, continued even when we were empty nesters. The only adjustments were the girls had to work their travel schedules, and they also contributed more as we split dinner, movie and birthday cake costs.

Game Nights: Less extravagant, but still enjoyable, were our low to no cost traditions at the house. The extent of our game nights varied over the years, but ultimately, we dedicated time to share in family activities on weekends and holidays when opportunities arose. We played all types of board games, card games and video games over the years.

The types of board games included Monopoly, Clue, Scrabble, Risk, Trivial Pursuit and The Game of Life, to name a few. Each of us had our favorites and ones we (sort of) dreaded. For example, the girls nor Vambie were overly excited when I choose Risk as the game for the evening. Jaelin dreaded Monopoly, Vambie liked Scrabble, but the game we probably played the most was Clue. In fact, we bought Video Clue to increase the variety of that game, although the original board game remained our staple.

Playing video games was a family event after we bought Wii. When the girls were young, they would watch me play games, but eventually I stopped playing, and / or they lost interest. But when we bought the Wii, not only did Jaleah and I play for father-daughter time, we collectively played various Wii four-person games so we all could participate and enjoy.

Another type of game we often played were card games. For our family, the more specific game was Bid Whist. And I freely admit, this did not neatly fall into the "just so we can have fun" category. This had broader implications.

Bid Whist is like advanced Spades. I also heard it is like Euchre, for those not familiar with the game. Basically, it is an advanced partner-based card game. Further, there is not an abundance of people who know how to play. However, I am an avid player. Vambie also knows how to play, as do both of my parents. My mom, in particular, is as avid a Bid Whist player as I am. So, when the girls were rather young (before the age of ten), and even before they knew how to play Spades, I began teaching them how to play Bid Whist.

As part of my instruction, I gave them tips about what card players like, and more importantly don't like. I told them card players don't like to play with those who are slow, nor those who don't know what they are doing, and really don't like to play with those who are slow and don't know what they are doing. After a few years of instruction and family game nights, I established a "tea-time" tradition with Grandma Liz (my mom). This meant any time we spent at least one night with Grandma, the four of us would play Bid Whist. The "tea" part was reflective of having hot tea while playing Bid Whist, though wine ended up being the preferred beverage for my mom. Over time the girls got old enough to both enjoy the card game and the wine. Also, every now and again, Vambie and / or my dad would join in and play, which made the evening that much more fun.

New Traditions: There were several new family traditions started in preparation for the girls leaving the house. The new routines were more so intended to maintain the Core 4 relationships and connectivity. This included our annual stock take, definitive reset of expectations regarding communication and an established "Christmas Break" routine. The beginning of college for Jaelin was the start of some of these, but the departure of Jaleah to college kicked in the full suite.

The annual stock take was / is a family sit-down whereby all four of us openly express our current mental, physical, emotional, financial, academic / professional and spiritual standing. We also talk about family, sibling relationships, our marriage, upcoming career changes and goals for the next year. We typically do this over an hour or so, and we go to each family member. I start and tell everyone where I am professionally, what my take is on the past year, and how I am in the noted areas. I then talk about my parents, brothers and sisters and their family, mindful that it is not for discussion outside the Core 4. This generates our understanding of the status of our nieces, nephews, cousins, aunts, uncles and other extended family that we have interacted with over the past several months. Vambie reluctantly gives her status and tells everyone about her side of the family similar to what I did for mine. Then each of the girls goes over where they are across the stock take areas. This covers updates on school / work, relationships, current year frustrations and next year's expectations. This fosters an open, candid discussion amongst all of us—and although no one likes the term, and initially everyone is reluctant, by the time we finish we all have a good understanding of the state of our family, individually and collectively.

It was during one of these sessions, the one preceding Jaleah starting college, that I explained that after that point, we would not have three to four months of sustained time together again. Because Jaelin was going to be seeking internships that following summer, and Jaleah would be doing the same soon thereafter, the schedules simply would not align for more than a few weeks at most in the future. This reality, obvious but necessary to be stated, created a new dynamic.

Due to the geographic separation and uncertainty of how often any one of us would talk to another, I announced that everyone should assume that if one person in the family was told, everyone else would know. Up to this point, sibling discussion, or father-daughter talks, may stay between those in the conversation or discretely be shared with the other parent (not to be voiced to the child who thought only the person they told knew). When they were children, sustaining that façade was okay, but as adults, that false premise would be problematic. This resetting of expectations now allowed for relatively disjointed conversations to coalesce into common family knowledge without anyone getting into their feelings about a secret being disclosed. For our family, this complemented the annual stock take and allowed me to have conversations less often with my girls but remain fully engaged in what is going on in their lives through Vambie.

Another routine I incorporated after they left for college was annual one-on-one lunches where we had dedicated father-daughter talks about how things were going during Christmas or Thanksgiving breaks. I primarily did this during Christmas due to available time, but it was a priority on my schedule and was essentially mandatory. It allowed me to get a feel for how school was going, ask about their relationships, discern their challenges as well as their concerns. I also got to mentor them about what is forthcoming whether upon graduation, upcoming internships, money or any other topic that naturally came up. It was intentionally relaxed and oriented to share conversations about my life and interests as well as theirs.

Vambie also directed that because we had girls, we had to stay invested for at least two years after they graduate college and are on their own. This was slightly longer than I had in mind. To me, the day after college graduation was a good mark but I understood the reason to extend beyond that. We had invested a lot to set them up for success, to attain a good credit score, to own their own vehicle, live in their own place and excel in whatever job they earned. Also, the first couple of years being fully independent can be a little unsettling for a twenty-one- or twenty-two-year-old. Therefore, during Jaelin's senior year, after she received an offer letter and accepted her job, the preparation for full transition began in earnest. This included car shopping, apartment shopping and furniture shopping. We had active talks about establishing new loans, getting more credit cards, budget management, how much to invest and overall lifestyle management in her new location. We discussed all of this with her, but we left the decisions up to her. Although we gave our perspective so she did not set herself up for struggles months or years down the road, it was on her to wade into the water of full functional independence.

The stories associated with the transition to full independence are unique to my girls' personalities but suffice to say it was not simple nor boring (particularly for Jaelin). Depending on the area, Vambie or I took the lead to assist and guide; but most importantly, Jaelin was fully attentive and responsive. She trusted our advice because, to that point, it had worked out well for her. For us, the best way to deal with a given situation was an adult-based conversation where she had full decision authority. We did not force our opinion on her because it was her money that she saved over the years, her signing bonus, her steady income and her lifestyle. We fostered all of this from her youth, and it was simply a continuation of the relationships built for nearly her entire life. It was not coincidental or happenstance.

We will replicate this with Jaleah, although tailor it to her personality, geographic location and money situation. Most will be similar because she is saving money from paid internships and has accepted a job offer where she will make a similar amount of money as her sister immediately upon graduation. Our girls are not the same, however, so we will work their situations based on their circumstance. We will best ensure each is positioned to be successful as we have striven to do since both were young.

In general, I sought to create an internal family dynamic that is conducive for enjoying each other's company and expressing ourselves. One where we can laugh at one another's jokes and be relaxed in each other's presence. The various games we played and activities we shared established a home and family setting that everyone wanted to be in and around. Such an environment contributes to our mutual respect and comfort as adults to talk about light-hearted and serious topics alike. Both of which are important for long-standing, healthy adult relations.

Head of Household

Some of us had fathers who were physically present; others had ones who were absent (sometimes even when physically present). Either way, we were profoundly affected by the presence or absence of our father. I titled this section *head of household* purposefully. The distinguishing characteristic between a father and head of household is the head of household is present in the house and dictates the direction of the family from a point of physical, mental and emotional presence. Though both demand acknowledgement of responsibility, the head of household is unquestionably in a leadership position. We are leaders of our house, and responsible for all that happens within it. A key tenet to leading is setting the conditions, and this starts with having and expressing your philosophy. As a parenting story, it is not my intent to write about being a good husband; however, you cannot neatly separate when writing about being head of household. I pray that every father accepts responsibility and invests the time and energy to perform as a husband (when applicable) and head of his household.

For the family, you provide the direction and guidance that your wife and children follow. You must decide how you want your family to function. This includes, at a minimum, the tone of communication, financial priorities and expectations of the children in and after high school. Once decided, openly discuss with your wife to ensure a common understanding of each critical area to allow for adherence throughout the relationship and as the family grows. If there is a disagreement, demand resolution—and regardless of who compromises, make certain the decision is implemented. Identify those transition points and reassess the state of the family. The birth of a child is clearly such a point; but throughout each child's growth, other transition points will emerge. As the head of household, proactively discuss what the ramifications of the major change is on you and the family. These can include career changes, location change, beginning of middle and high school as well as empty nest. Some are more obvious than others, but each can significantly affect how the family functions, and therefore warrant updated direction and guidance to ensure family goals remain attainable.

Regarding recognizing, or not recognizing, transition points, I offer an example. I admit that adjusting to a given transition point was a parental weakness of mine for many years. This weakness crystalized in 2005, and I realized that I must do better in anticipating the breadth and depth of change so that the family does not unnecessarily endure the turbulence. I was in Kansas at the time, and what seemed like a simple change was occurring over the summer. I was selected for a military school, but all it entailed was me driving to a different location on the installation, or so it seemed. As I transitioned from a normal day-to-day job to an academic schedule, the difference in time and energy management emerged. Working a normal job meant when I was done with work, all my time was available for me, Vambie, the girls and activities of interest. While simply working, I picked Jaleah up from gymnastics (which was thirty-five minutes away), was an assistant coach for soccer, mentored / tutored locally and was active in the local church. A few weeks into an academic schedule, I had reading and writing assignments, had to do school-based activities, had less time to relax and fundamentally had an altered energy and time management framework. This reads like a no-brainer, but I was slow to recognize and adapt. I started getting frustrated because I was trying to do all I had been doing, while doing more homework, which was not working. Eventually, I snapped when Vambie asked me to pick up Jaleah from gymnastics. I soon realized it was my fault that I allowed my schedule to overwhelm me, and I apologized to Vambie for getting upset and pushing back on taking an hour out of my schedule to get one of our girls because she was cooking dinner. I eventually scaled back on the list of activities to which I committed myself so I could re-establish the necessary work-life balance. I also started reading in the living room; I told Vambie that if ever she wanted to talk, I would pause reading because I did not want to separate myself from her or the girls during the academic year. These were simple and easy adjustments, but they exemplify the responsibility I had to make the transition calm for everyone, recognizing that it started with me.

Another definitive head of household responsibility is defining acceptable behavior by our children, which directly reflects what you allow. At an early age, children will interpret the "left and right limits" and push to expand those limits as a matter of being a teenager. Although there is no book on how to manage the specifics of your relationship, it should be in the best interest of the family. Seeds are planted early in your relationship and you will dictate the energy invested to maintain the communication, respect and trust-level through adulthood. Do not expect your children to lead or initiate conversations about sensitive and confusing topics as that is your responsibility. Boy or girl, the relationship with the father is unique and special; similarly, the absence of such a relationship is far-reaching and potentially destructive.

This reveals a reality nearly everyone experiences. As each one of us has a story, and it usually begins with reference to our biological parents. Whether conceived by accident or planned, naturally or medically aided, in love or in lust, eventually a baby is introduced into the world. Upon arrival, that young child is welcomed by whomever is present at the time. That may be one or both parents, who are young or old, excited or worried, prepared or ill-equipped. Regardless of the circumstance, a child's story begins, of which they have no control of their situation, no choice in who raises them, and no idea what good or bad parenting is. Consciously and subconsciously, the mental, physical and emotional foundation is formed that creates a baseline through adulthood. This near universal scenario gives a glimpse of the awesome impact of a present, or absent, father.

Prayer and Patience

Faith, defined by Hebrews 11:1, is the substance of things hoped for, the evidence of things not seen. Obviously, this definition is with respect to God, but faith has applicability to us as parents as well. We need to have faith in God, to help guide us through all the trials and tribulations that our family will endure, but we also must have faith in our parental approach. We must trust what we are doing, that the decisions we make and the actions we take will yield the results we desire. Be humbled by the responsibilities we have and acknowledge that we are not alone in this endeavor. Prayer is powerful, and we should use it to the fullest extent possible. Trust ourselves and believe in our children and understand there are circumstances we cannot control or foresee. In those times, prayer and faith become paramount.

I recall a story my dad told me regarding his answer to a question he was asked about how he raised four children, none of whom had alcohol, drug or criminal issues. His response was love and a lot of prayer. This culminating part of the book ties together how my own prayer and patience is the driver to being the head of my household. How it sustained me through challenging times when I was uncertain if the course I chose, or the decision I made, was the right one. As parents, we cannot predict the future, nor how our children will react to situations we may create. As the head of household, our decisions encompass more than just our children; they affect everyone individually and collectively. My professional situation is a factor; Vambie's comfort with the environment is a consideration— and multiple facets that our girls may not appreciate across the academic, athletic and social arenas matter. It was important to instill ownership, and not foster an "it was your fault" that I am not doing as well as I could because of what you (parents) did. This was not always possible as we transitioned from place to place, and if an "it was your fault" attitude consumed either of our girls, it would have created a negative disposition that affected their view on teenage life, high school and linger into post-high school perspectives. Therefore, we challenged them to take ownership of where they were in life and what they could do to make the situation best for them. We challenged them to not blame anyone for the situation that develops from this circumstance if it doesn't work the way they want, and that they can define what will occur by their attitude and work effort. This exemplified the patience model that helped me trust myself and portray that trust to my girls with the hope they also trust themselves. This may not be obvious initially. In fact, it may take months or years to fully realize. But over time, it can be demonstrated that things did work out.

I have a strong relationship with my Lord and Savior, and I routinely communicate with the Holy Spirit to guide me. There are many decisions I made with long-term ramifications that cannot be foreseen. Whatever faith you may have, assuming you do, and whatever relationship with God you have, seek guidance when you are faced with difficult decisions. Vambie and I both are prayerful; once we decided on a course of action for the house, we trusted that decision. More importantly, we did not second guess ourselves. We put all our energy into dealing with the situations we created for ourselves and making the decision we made work.

We made religion a part of our girls' lives at an early age. We have been in places where we were active in the local church and other places where we were inactive. During the critical shaping years, we made a point to find a church that had a good children's church and we leveraged that setting to teach key lessons grounded in our faith. The lessons learned during that time, and the positive impressions religion had on them served as a reference for later conversations. It also embedded in them traits that we desired, such as respect, selflessness and willingness to support activities. My girls applied these lessons by reaching out to those who weren't as popular or welcoming new members to their respective team.

I tend to be reflective by nature—and with that, I consciously had my girls look back and understand their achievements. Part of building self-esteem is to internalize your value, and a contributing factor is realizing your successes. This is more than lauding them when they do well in real-time but forcing them to look back at what they overcame. They should be able to appreciate how well they did academically, athletically or in activities and own those achievements. I note ownership because it is not about what we as parents did to enable them, but for them to realize their role and importance. At one point, I told Jaelin, "Don't give me credit for your success. Many people get advice and do nothing with it; you used it to your benefit. Similarly, you shouldn't blame me for your failures." This was in response to her attributing success in math to me, but I needed her to internalize that success regardless of the merits of her appreciation.

I used different approaches to create this reflective dynamic such as having everyone write down their goals for the upcoming year and keeping them in envelopes until the following New Year's Eve when we talked about the successes of the previous year. I also had them write down their favorite schools, teachers, coaches, sports, friends, places we lived and why they ranked where they ranked. This fostered frank discussion on both positive things and those more challenging things over the past eight to ten years. It also caused them to express thoughts, reasoning and memories that they could reference years later when they have to overcome situations.

Recalling personal success and failures as a reference point is good, but from a parental perspective, there should not be a question of our love and pride. I tend to highlight the negative in situations versus noting the positive. I did this in my profession, and I carried it over to my family. The good thing is I realized this; although I worked on it, I tended to not display or say how proud I was of my girls on a routine basis. For children, I believe they adjust to our personality and assume however they are parented is the way they will be parented which includes not expecting to be lauded by their father (in this instance). My solution for this characteristic was to write letters to my girls every few years that were explicitly positive (as I have shared throughout the book) to express my love and pride for their development. I do not know if they kept these letters, but I know I became prouder and more appreciative of the potential of my girls as I wrote them.

The balance between family and professional responsibilities, satisfying the wife while feeling empowered as a man and attaining individual joy and happiness is not inherently easy. Further, the dynamic is ever changing as you, the wife and the children, are each transforming at varying rates. Every family is unique based on several variables that cannot be addressed in any book. Consider seeking a mentor who you respect and has traveled a similar road that you desire. Be honest with the mentor and welcome advice that you can evaluate and apply based on your situation. The challenge is so stark that masking and avoiding it can ultimately lead to disappointment. Look at yourself as a start point, and assess what you can do to improve as a husband and father. This extends to the expectations of your wife. You need to change before you ask your wife to change. I made a list of the seven major issues Vambie had with me as a husband, and I dedicated myself to do better about ten years in (yes, it took me a few years to have this revelation). This required acknowledging I was flawed, then a decision to make changes and ultimately actions to demonstrate those changes. I was honest with myself and eventually, those improvements caused Vambie to change too.

In writing this book, I pray every parent who reads it recognizes the power they have to positively impact the lives of those they should cherish the most, their children. That everyone of us owns our responsibility and appreciates that our children did not ask to come into this world—that was our decision. That our children have no control over how well, or poorly, they are raised—that is on us. That our children will reflect us as parents, the good and the bad, in youth and as adults—and that is because of us.

If a new parent, and you were wondering what the next decade or so will entail, hopefully this book gave you some insights. I pray it demonstrated that any parent can get in front, and stay there, by being deliberate and proactive. And encourages you to have a plan, early on, and adjust from a common place of reference as your child grows. Because we as parents, regardless of situation or circumstance, have an obligation to forthrightly equip our children to reach their full potential and enable them to attain peace and joy.

For us men, I believe there are differences between being a boy, being a man, being a husband, being a father and being the head of household. And there is no guarantee we will understand those differences when it is most important. I have been fortunate to realize success in several respects, and my charge is to share the lessons with others. My success as a father was reflected in a letter I received with my Father's Day card in 2018. It touched my heart and soul as my girls articulated the impact I had on their lives as young adults. It is a sentiment I pray every father would receive from their sons or daughters when they reach a similar point.

Father,

Over the past 21 to 22 years of your life, it is an understatement to say that we are merely proud of you. Words cannot describe the immense impact you have had on our lives from small instances like your life nuggets, that at the time we didn't know the weight it would carry in our future decisions, or moments or traditions like you and I going to Applebee's to get dessert or you and me walking every Sunday just to talk. Having the ability to balance two amazingly talented and intelligent children, one flawless wife (but a bit crazy), and a military career spanning over 25 years (we think), it is only fair to say that you are nothing short of remarkable. Over these years there is no other image of a father that either of us wish to have. You are wise beyond your years, intelligent beyond normal capacity, understanding in times of confusion for us, and above all hilarious when we need laughter even if neither of us know we do. The definition of a father and a man in many dictionaries is very finite, but because of you what we see as a father and a man is something so immaculate no one who crosses our path will ever compare. You may not be perfect James Edward White Jr., but on this Father's Day in the year 2018 you are, at least to us (the only people that matter), a perfect father.

Love your 2nd and 3rd favorite people in the World.

Jaelin and Jaleah White

Jaelin White   *Jaleah White*

ACKNOWLEDGMENTS

Vambie—for being my soulmate and helpmate in this, and in my life.
Katie—for being there from the first draft.
Pam—for helping me get this across the finish line.
Family, friends and supporters who helped and encouraged me throughout this endeavor.

ABOUT THE AUTHOR

Raised in Western Pennsylvania, graduate of the University of Georgia (BS Chemistry), masters from Kansas State University (MS Adult Continuing Education), U.S. Army Officer of 25+ years and owner of JED White, LLC. A humble servant, passionate about positively affecting the lives of children by enabling parents to be empowered and effective.

Made in the USA
Middletown, DE
03 August 2019